Using the
Futures, Forwards and Options
Markets

By the same author
Foreign Exchange and
the Corporate Treasurer

Using the Futures, Forwards and Options Markets

JOHN HEYWOOD

Adam and Charles Black
LONDON

First published 1984
A & C Black (Publishers) Ltd
35 Bedford Row, London WC1R 4JH

Heywood, John, *1940*-
    Using the futures, forwards and options markets.
    1. Money market
    I. Title
    332.1   HG226

    ISBN 0-7136-2617-8

ISBN 0-7136-2617-8

Filmset in Monophoto Times New Roman by
Latimer Trend & Company Ltd, Plymouth
Printed and bound in Great Britain by
A. Wheaton & Co Ltd, Exeter, Devon

Contents

Acknowledgements

I should like to thank my colleagues in the dealing room at Hambros Bank who have helped me to clarify ideas on these subjects by means of our constant debate and discussion of any new aspect of the market; I would particularly like to mention Bob Thomas, Ken Williams, Graham Steward, Tim Humphreys, Richard Cooley, and Sarah Greg. It is largely by means of these debates that I believe we all learn together as the market develops, although obviously the best way to learn about a market is to actually use it and then to test our ideas against the sober criteria of the profit and loss account.

I would not wish to imply that such discussion has been entirely internal, and I should therefore also like to recognise the assistance and ideas from many customers, banks, brokers, and other market participants in Europe and the USA, and members of the staffs of the London International Financial Futures Exchange, and the Currency Options division of the Philadelphia Stock Exchange, Inc.

For Richard and Louise

Introduction

Throughout the late 1970s and the early 1980s short-term financial markets have become more and more volatile. This has been true for both interest rates and exchange rates and has also been true whether measured by size of movements occurring, or by speed of movement, or even by frequency of movement. These developments have had a serious impact upon the profitability and even the survival of many businesses. This newly hostile business environment has led directly to a number of innovations in financial markets which have a common defensive theme – protecting businesses against risk.

In respect of foreign exchange risk there has been a substantial growth in the use of forward markets and a parallel change in the sophistication with which these traditional techniques have been used. Entirely new techniques and markets have also come into existence over the past few years, most notably the new markets in currency options.

In respect of interest rate risk, the development of futures markets in the USA and more recently in London is of growing significance for treasury management. It seems inevitable that these markets will continue to grow and that treasurers and aspiring treasurers will increasingly seek to become familiar with them.

This book is intended to provide an introduction and reference source for all those working in industry or in financial institutions and banks who may be concerned with these problems, as well as being a general text on the subject for use by colleges and business schools.

There of course exists a considerable volume of technical literature about these markets already, but much of it is intended for existing market professionals and assumes considerable prior knowledge. Further, options literature does not usually tell a potential user when it might be cheaper or more appropriate to use futures instead, let alone some of each, and futures literature may well treat futures only. This book results from the recognition that there still seems to be a lack of general, plain English, explanatory material about how these markets work, how to use them, and which might be the most appropriate to use in a given situation. Accordingly this book attempts to cover the futures, forwards, and options markets, and how to use them either separately or in conjunction with one another to optimum effect – options together with forwards, or forwards together with futures and so on. Use of all these techniques is much assisted by a knowledge of technical analysis and technical trading methods; these techniques are also introduced.

I have no love of market jargon and believe we could operate without most of it perfectly well. Indeed, I am aware that much of the apparent difficulty surrounding the subject is simply a language problem – it disappears once the technical jargon has been explained. But so long as market operators use the jargon others must know what it means; key technical terms are therefore introduced where relevant as part of the general aim of demystifying the subject. A fuller guide to the terminology of the markets may be found in the Glossary. For those whose interest may have been stimulated by reading this book, the Bibliography provides suggestions for further in-depth coverage of particular aspects.

Finally, there is a table of data facing the first page of text. Table A, which consists of foreign exchange, interest, and futures rates as at 4 January 1983. Frequent reference is made to this Table, the rates being used in many of the examples in the text.

TABLE A

MARKET RATES ON 4 JANUARY 1983

Foreign Exchange Rates Currency	Code	Spot Exchange/$	3 month Prem/Dis	6 month Interest Rate
Pound Sterling*	GBP	1·6270/75	49/45	$10\frac{1}{2}/10\frac{3}{8}$
German Mark	DEM	2·3563/68	187/183	$6\frac{1}{8}/5\frac{7}{8}$
French Franc	FRF	6·6725/800	3000/3075	25/24
Netherlands Guilder	NLG	2·6030/50	253/248	$5\frac{1}{2}/\frac{3}{8}$
Italian Lira	ITL	1358·50/9·50	6100/6600	26/25
Swiss Franc	CHF	1·9780/95	283/277	$3\frac{5}{8}/\frac{1}{2}$
Swedish Krona	SEK	7·2435/55	530/550	$12\frac{1}{4}/12$
Norwegian Krone	NOK	6·9680/700	870/910	$14\frac{3}{8}/\frac{1}{8}$
Canadian Dollar	CAD	1·2278/81	21/26	$10\frac{1}{4}/10$
Hong Kong Dollar	HKD	6·5120/70	70/20	$9/8\frac{5}{8}$
Saudi Riyal	SAR	3·4403/08	198/153	$8\frac{1}{4}/7\frac{1}{2}$
Kuwaiti Dinar*	KWD	3·4590/610	N.A.	$9\frac{3}{4}/8\frac{3}{4}$
Australian Dollar*	AUD	0·9855/60	50/35	$11\frac{3}{4}/\frac{1}{4}$
Japanese Yen	JPY	228·85/95	1·34/1·28	$6\frac{3}{4}/\frac{1}{2}$

* Reciprocal rate, quoted as USD per unit of currency.
Currency codes are International Standards Organisation Codes, as used by international banks.

Eurodollar rates, % per annum. (offered side, bid side $\frac{1}{8}$ lower throughout)

Day to day	1 month	2 months	3 months	4 months	5 months	6 months	over drafts
$9\frac{1}{8}$	$9\frac{1}{8}$	$9\frac{1}{8}$	$9\frac{1}{8}$	$9\frac{3}{16}$	$9\frac{1}{4}$	$9\frac{5}{16}$	$9\frac{1}{8}$

LIFFE Futures Rates

Contract	March Delivery	June Delivery
3 Month Eurodollar	91·12	90·76
Short Sterling Interest	90·45	90·31
Long Gilt	103·30	103·12
Sterling Exchange Rate	1·6235	1·6235
Deutsche Mark Exchange Rate	42·63	42·96

1 Forward FX Markets

1.1 Introduction to Currency Risk

The first requirement of any book having currency risk management as a major concern must surely be to make a realistic assessment of the scale of the problem, based on the actual facts of the market. For some reason this is seldom done.

The table on p. 2 shows the percentage variation between the high and low experienced during an average year for some of the principal world currencies. The table is the average of actual market experience over each of the ten years 1973 to 1982 inclusive. The data is surprisingly consistent. Very roughly there will be something like a 18% swing in a typical year between the high and low of a major exchange rate. In a bad year it may be twice as great as this; in a good year only around a half of the average.

It is worth noting that the worst year in the period is not the same for the different currencies. In fact the most volatile year for dollar/sterling was 1981, for dollar/DMark it was 1973, for dollar/yen it was 1978, and for sterling/Norwegian it was 1976. So it is not just some years that are particularly bad for all currencies, in any given year it may be relied upon that some exchange rate or another will prove to be very volatile.

But why bother to show a sterling/Norwegian rate anyway? After all, this is perhaps not a very important currency compared with the others shown in the table. It is partly to demonstrate that it is not solely the major currencies that experience these large movements; the smaller currencies do so too. But it is also to show that we are not simply obtaining a measure of the volatility of the dollar – the dollar is not involved in the sterling versus Norwegian rate, yet the volatility turns out just the same as the others.

EXCHANGE RATE VOLATILITY
% variation high v low during year

Rate	Average 1973–1981	Biggest	Smallest
£/$	18	35	9
DM/$	18	39	7
Yen/$	16	26	5
NK/£	17	36	7

Planning basis say 20%

Many currencies tend to move together in groups, such as the continental currencies, or perhaps the US dollar and the Canadian dollar. They will tend to move in tandem against currencies outside their group, and move relative to each other by smaller amounts. As an initial rule of thumb, these intra-group movements, for instance Deutsche mark versus Netherlands guilder, or US dollar versus Canadian dollar, are about half the size of inter-group movements such as Deutsche mark versus US dollar.

It may then be considered a reasonable planning basis to assume that we will get around a 20% movement in a year on a major inter-group exchange rate and around 10% on an intra-group exchange rate. The most obvious fact about these numbers is that they are far larger than the swings companies usually allow for in their budgeting process. Treasurers might legitimately enquire why this is.

Of course 20% per annum in no way implies 5% every three months. Normally, experience is that the markets go through doldrum periods followed by large, relatively sudden movements. The history of the matter is again reasonably consistent; one can expect half the year's total movement to occur in one quarter. We can even construct a second table showing the proportion of the total

% of year's total movement likely to occur	
In 3 months	50%
In 1 month	30%
In 1 week	20%

year's movement likely to occur during a quarter, or a month, or a week.

So experience tells us that, assuming we take 20% as a pointer of a typical year's movement, we ought reasonably to expect during one quarter of the year to see a 10% movement, and that during one of the months of the year we will see a 6% movement and that during one of the weeks we will see a 4% movement.

This is in no way contingency planning; it is the most likely outcome if markets simply continue to behave in the same way as they have done for the past decade. Of course, we also know, or should know, that if we hit a bad patch, movements can be double these average figures. Wishing the numbers were smaller will not make them so; doing cash flow projections allowing for 5% variations in exchange rates is just not facing reality.

We must learn to manage the currency risks inherent in the business; we now start that learning process with the basics of the FX market.

1.2   Value Dating

A foreign exchange contract is an agreement to exchange a bank balance in one currency for a bank balance in another currency:

- on an agreed date
- at an agreed rate

The agreed date is a vital component of the contract. Most commonly the value date is 'value spot' or two days ahead from the date of the deal, but any date further away than the spot date is considered to be a 'forward'. There is no difference in principle between a spot and forward deal other than the difference in the agreed date of settlement and the consequent modification to the rate to reflect the difference in the date. The nature of the rate modification required is the matter we turn to next.

1.3   Price Calculation for Forward Contracts

There has been a widespread belief amongst the business community that forward exchange rates are created by some arcane mixture of alchemy and economic forecasting. These rates by contrast are arrived at by the very simplest of arithmetic and without the slightest element of forecasting being required.

DERIVATION OF FORWARD RATES

Starting Exchange rate   DM/£ = 4·2650

	£		DM
Starting amount	1,000	or	4,2650
3 month interest rate	$12\frac{3}{4}\%$		$8\frac{3}{4}\%$
Proceeds after 3 months	1·0319	or	4·3583
		↘ratio↙	
Forward Exchange rate		4·2236 DM/£	
Difference from spot, or Premium		4·14 pfennig	

The principles are perhaps most easily understood by means of the type of illustration shown in the table 'Derivation of Forward Rates'. We assume that the spot rate between DMarks and sterling is 4·2650. Now, any citizen of the United Kingdom is perfectly free to continue to hold one pound or to go and convert it into DM 4·2650 at his free choice. Further, at current interest rates he is able to obtain $12\frac{3}{4}\%$ per annum for 3 month deposits in sterling, or, alternatively, $8\frac{3}{4}\%$ per annum for 3 month deposits in DM.

Comparing his two possible investment strategies for the 3 month period then, he may either:

  a: place one pound on deposit and finish up with GBP 1·0319, or

  b: convert his pound into DM 4·2650 and place the marks on deposit for the period to finish up with DM 4·3583.

Dividing both maturity amounts by 1·0319, we now see that for every pound he could have at maturity he could instead have DM 4·3583/1·0319 = DM 4·2236. This 4·2236 is the forward exchange rate.

If the reader is surprised by this, then he should consider how very much more surprising it would be if this were not the forward exchange rate. For in that case our investor would be able to sell his maturing marks at the true forward rate and make a profit versus option (*a*). Sadly, there are no free gifts left lying about in the international foreign exchange markets!

The above example clearly made no reference to market forecasts of any kind. Nor should it be assumed that forward rates imply any such forecast. A moment's thought will demonstrate why this is the case. Suppose that in the above sterling interest rates were to be substantially increased. The forward rate would fall to a lower figure than DM 4·2236, implying sterling weaker forward than before. Yet when this actually happened, and sterling interest rates were raised by the new Thatcher government, the market's forecast was, reasonably enough, that sterling would be stronger over the months ahead. So the forward rate, a calculation showing a weaker forward price than spot, was not even showing a movement in the same direction as market forecasts, or indeed subsequent events, for some 18 months.

1.4 Quotation of Exchange Rates

Foreign exchange markets generally quote currencies as a rate against the US dollar, most currencies being quoted as units of currency per US dollar. Sterling, Australian dollar and one or two other currencies are, however, quoted as US dollars per unit of the base currency. In the more usual case of, say, the DMark, the quote for spot delivery may for instance be –

2·3120/30

Here the 'quoted' currency is the DMark and the 'base' currency is the US dollar. 'Buy' or 'sell' always refers to the quoted currency; never the base. The selling price is always quoted first, and is of course always the lower of the two figures. Here the bank sells DMarks at 2·3120 and buys at 2·3130.

In the above example of 2·3120/30 the '1', being the cents figure, is referred to as the 'big figure'; and the 20 and 30, which are 100ths of a cent, are referred to as 'points'. This rate may be quoted between dealers as 'twenty thirty on one', or 'I make you twenty thirty on a big figure of one'. The initial 2·3 will be assumed to be known by everybody and will only be mentioned in conclusion of the deal by way of confirmation.

Sterling is quoted in all centres as a price of US dollars per pound. Thus the dollar is treated as the currency being bought and sold against a sterling base. Therefore a quote of 1·6020/25 means that the bank sells dollars at 1·6020 and buys dollars at 1·6025.

Forward prices may be quoted as outright prices or as premia. The outright price looks in format precisely the same as a spot price, but simply refers to a different delivery date. For instance, the DMark rate for 3 months forward might be, say, 2·3030/45. But there is a second convention whereby the forward premium, being simply the difference between the spot and forward prices, is quoted by itself. For instance, if our spot price was still 2·3120/30, the forward premium would be quoted as 90/85 points:

$$2·3030/45 = 2·3120/30 - 90/85$$
Outright = Spot   – Premium

Negative premia are called discounts. A currency having a lower interest rate than the dollar stands at a premium against the dollar, being more expensive than spot; a currency having a higher interest rate than the dollar stands at a discount against the dollar. Strictly, a currency at a discount should be quoted as:

$$+70/+85$$

In practice, plus and minus signs are usually omitted because the sign may be deduced from the following rule:

    Bigger figure first = premium
    Smaller figure first = discount

Here 90/85 indicates premium, 70/85 indicates discount.

The reader may wish to use this section as a self test on the material presented in **1.4** above. For those who wish to consult them the answers are listed at the end of the questions. The basic data on which the questions and answers are based is given in Table A, on page xii.

1 *a*: What is the 'big figure' in the FRF rate?
   b: What is the spread?
   c: Is the forward FRF at a premium or a discount?

2 Which of the following pairs of currencies is worth more?
   a: USD 1 or AUD 1?
   b: USD 1 or CAD 1?
   c: CAD 1 or AUD 1?

3 Calculate the following middle spot prices. (Use the average between the sell and buy prices shown.)
  a: Saudi Riyals/Kuwaiti Dinar
  b: Norwegian Kroner/Pound Sterling
  c: Italian Lira/Netherlands Guilder
4 Calculate middle exchange rate for the Swiss franc/dollar:
  a: spot
  b: 3 months forward
  c: 6 months forward. (Hint: use method in **1**.3)
5 Calculate middle exchange rate for Swedish krona/sterling:
  a: spot
  b: 3 months forward
  c: 6 months forward

Answers
1 *a*: The big figure is 7
  b: The spread is 75 points
  c: Discount. (Forwards quoted small figure first.)
2 *a*: USD
  b: USD
  c: AUD. (Worth USD 0·98575, whereas CAD is worth USD 0·81437.)
3 *a*: 3·44055 × 3·46 = 11·9043 SAR/KWD
  b: 6·9690 × 1·62725 = 11·3403 NOK/GBP
  c: 1359/2·6040 = 521·89 ITL/NLG
4 *a*: 1·9787 CHF/USD
  b: 1·9787 − 0·0280 = 1·9507 CHF/USD
  c: 6 month CHF interest rate = 3·5625% pa
    6 month USD interest rate = $9\frac{5}{16} - \frac{1}{16} = 9·250$
    1 USD invested for 6 months becomes USD 1·04625
    1 CHF invested for 6 months becomes CHF 1·0178125
    6 month rate = 1·9787 × 1·0178125/1·04625
          = 1·9249 CHF/USD
5 *a*: 7·2445 × 1·62725 = 11·7886 SEK/GBP
  b: 3 month SEK/USD = 7·2445 + 0·0540 = 7·2985
    3 month USD/GBP = 1·62725 − 0·0047 = 1·62255
    3 month SEK/GBP = 7·2985 × 1·62255 = 11·8422

c: 6 month SEK interest rate = 12·125%
6 month GBP interest rate = 10·4375%
1 SEK invested for 6 months becomes SEK 1·060625
1 GBP invested for 6 months becomes GBP 1·0521875
6 month rate = 11·7886 × 1·060625/1·0521875
       = 11·8831 SEK/GBP

2 Arbitrage and Swap Transactions

2.1 Interest Arbitrage

Probably the simplest way to introduce this topic is by way of an example, using actual market rates. We will use rates as at 4 January 1983. The example assumes that a dealer is trying to determine whether he can 'produce' DEM to lend more cheaply by using the Eurodollar market and interest arbitrage, or by direct borrowing of DEM in the deposit market.

Data: Spot DEM/USD 2·3565
6 months premium 370 points
6 months Euro\$ $9\frac{5}{16}/3\frac{3}{16}$
6 months is currently 182 days

Calculation if borrow USD and convert to DEM:

  a: Borrow USD 1 million @ $9\frac{5}{16}\%$ for 182 days
    Interest cost = USD 47,080.
    USD sum required at maturity = USD 1,047,080.

  b: Outright rate DEM/USD = 2·3565 − 0·0370 = 2·3195
    To buy USD 1,047,080 @ 2·3195 will cost
    DEM1,047,080 × 2·3195 = DEM2,428,702
    This sum of DEM will be required at the maturity date.

  c: The sum of DEM that is available at the start date by conversion of the 1million dollars at the spot rate is:
    DEM1,000,000 × 2·3565 = DEM2,356,500

d: Sum in DEM to be earned as interest over the 6 months is the difference between these two DEM figures, ie:
DEM2,428,702 − 2,356,500 = DEM72,202

e: Expressed as a rate of interest on the DEM2,356,500 originally borrowed, this is:
$72,202 \times 360/182 \times 100/2,356,500 = 6\cdot0606\%$

This cost compares with the cost of borrowing the funds direct at the slightly higher market rate of $6\cdot125\%$

2.2 Interrelationship of FX and Eurocurrency Markets

There are two key facts to note about the result of the calculation above. Firstly, the two answers of $6\cdot0606\%$ and $6\cdot125\%$ are very close to one another. Secondly, they are not the same.

The reason why they are very close to one another is not hard to see. We saw in Chapter 1 that forward exchange rates were derived from the difference between the interest rates of the two currencies involved. All we are doing now is running the calculation in reverse – calculating one interest rate given the other rate and the forward exchange rate. Logically, then, our two answers should be identical.

So why aren't they identical? The first reason why they don't line up exactly is because market prices are not static quantities, they are in continuous movement. A physicist will tell you that the surface of the Atlantic Ocean should logically be precisely horizontal, and indeed if the surface were static and without outside disturbance due to wind and tide, so it would be. The only way in which parts of the surface can be higher than other parts is if they are in motion at the time. Even then, every individual portion of the surface will be endeavouring to return to equilibrium, the totally flat condition of the physicist. In the absence of any outside disturbance this would eventually be achieved.

Market prices behave similarly, continually being pushed away from their equilibrium condition by new outside disturbances; buyers or sellers. The equilibrium level may be overshot for a period, or may itself be moved by one-way market pressure. The likelihood of everything being precisely at equilibrium at any given time is extremely small.

There are other, more technical reasons why the market may not act to arbitrage away small differences between direct and interest arbitrage rates, allowing an 'arbitrage turn' to persist.

As we have seen, a bank having $ deposits but wishing to make DEM loans has two routes open to it:

  a: lend the $ to the market, and borrow the required DEM
    or
  b: convert the $ to DEM and lend the funds as DEM

Route (*a*) has some extra costs for a bank over route (*b*):

(i) The $ loan will use up part of Bank X's credit line to whichever bank takes the $. This represents an opportunity cost in that the bank may now have to turn down other potentially profitable business with this bank over the months to come.

(ii) The DEM borrowing will also use up part of the lending bank's credit line for Bank X. This is also an opportunity cost in that the lending bank will be able to conduct less other business with Bank X over the months to come.

(iii) Route (*a*) will increase the balance sheet by twice as much as route (*b*). This clearly affects balance sheet ratios including such aspects as liquidity ratios and capital adequacy ratios as well as management targets which may be defined in terms of return on total assets.

(iv) Both (*a*) and (*b*) involve transaction costs of dealing turns and possibly brokerage which will alter the relative attractiveness of the two routes as well as imposing a minimum cost for effecting the arbitrage.

For all the above reasons it is apparent that arbitrage turns will be created in the market, and that they are able to persist. On the other hand, if gaps become too big, it will become attractive to 'go round the triangle' and close the gap down.

2.3 'Cheap' Loans and Interest Rate Traps

There is an understandable belief that it must be attractive to take 'cheap' loans in foreign currencies. This has been perhaps most widespread in Swiss francs, where interest rates have been very low for some years.

The sort of argument is that exchange rates vary but are essentially unpredictable (so you may just as likely win or lose on that aspect) but the company will have a cast iron certainty of a saving in the interest rate of x% per annum, which is (in these difficult times for cash flow etc!) definitely worth having.

4 January 1981

A UK based company borrows CHF 1 million at $7\frac{1}{2}\%$ per annum for 2 years. CHF/GBP is 4·2286

Loan proceeds thus provide CHF 1,000,000/4·2286
= GBP 236,486

4 January 1982

After one year interest of CHF 75,000 is due.
CHF/GBP is now 3·4385

Interest cost = 75,000/3·4385
           = GBP 21,812

4 January 1983

The second interest payment is now due, along with repayment of the principal. CHF/GBP is now 3·2199

Interest cost for second year = 75,000/3·2199
                             = GBP 23,293

Repayment of principal   = 1,000,000/3·2199
                        = GBP 310,568

Capital loss   = GBP 310,568 − 236,486
                        = GBP   74,082

Analysis

	GBP	% of Amount borrowed
Interest year 1, 'coupon'	17,736	7·5
exchange loss	4,076	1·72
	21,812	
Interest year 2, 'coupon'	17,736	7·5
exchange loss	5,557	2·35
	23,293	
Capital loss	74,082	31·3
Total 2 year costs:		50·37%

If the capital loss is not allowable against tax, as is probable, then the cost rises to 50·37 + 31·3 = 81·67% or over 40% per annum.

Sadly, life is seldom this simple. The example on p. 13, using actual figures, illustrates the fallacies.

The example shows a number of alarming features of this type of transaction:

a: There is a capital loss over the two years of $31 \cdot 3\%$, or say $15\frac{1}{2}\%$ per annum. This alone would make it a very expensive transaction even if the interest rate were zero.

b: If the loan is in respect of a capital transaction, the Inland Revenue is unlikely to consider this capital loss as allowable against trading income for tax purposes. This effectively doubles the cost of the foreign exchange loss, to some 30% per annum, still without reckoning interest into the cost.

c: Although interest was set as $7\frac{1}{2}\%$ per annum, note that this is $7\frac{1}{2}\%$ of the original Swiss franc amount, not $7\frac{1}{2}\%$ of the amount of sterling this produced on drawdown. As shown in the analysis, this aspect, often not considered by treasurers, increases the interest cost in year 1 by $1 \cdot 72\%$ and in year 2 by $2 \cdot 35\%$. Actual interest rate was thus $9 \cdot 535\%$, more than 2% per annum higher than the nominal 'coupon' rate. Ironically, even the supposedly cast iron certain reduction in interest rates is not achieved.

The 'cheap' loan has its exact counterpart in the 'higher return' deposit. A classic example of this type of 'interest rate trap' is illustrated in the Norwegian krone example below.

INTEREST RATE TRAP — 14 May 1975

Situation
Company has $1 million for placement for three months. It has payments to make in US dollars at the end of this period. Should they place dollars on deposit at $6\frac{3}{8}\%$ or convert to Norwegian kroner and place those on deposit at the better rate of $8\frac{1}{4}\%$?

Outcome

    a: $1 million dollars placed on deposit for three months yields $1,015,937 at maturity, or

    b: on 14 May dollars could be converted to Norwegian kroner at 4·85 50. So after three months the company receives:

the principal	NK	4,855,000
+ interest		100,134
	NK	4,955,134

But after the three months was over, on 14 August 1975, the exchange rate had moved to NK$ = 5·46 00 so the proceeds amounted to –

$$\frac{4,955,134}{5·46\ 00} = \$907,534$$

Difference relative to option (*a*) $108,403

It will be seen that because of the subsequent fall of the Norwegian krone relative to the dollar during the three months, the company involved would have lost out by $108,403 representing a 43% per annum loss – and all incurred for the sake of trying to make 2%!

2.4 Return on all Currencies is equal after Cost of Cover

It is not of course certain that the outcome will turn out quite as bad as in the two examples just quoted, although it should be remembered that both examples are real case histories using actually experienced rates. It may even be comforting to imagine that it might be possible to gain the interest rate advantage and then to protect against the exchange risk by covering forward, so obtaining the best of both worlds. But alas, there are no free gifts!

Reverting to the earlier Swiss franc example, the borrowing rate was $7\frac{1}{2}\%$. Let us suppose that, at the time, the rate in GBP would have been $12\frac{1}{2}\%$, or 5% higher. What would have been the cost of foreign exchange cover at this time? The cost of cover is equal to the interest differential, i.e. 5%. This leads directly to two discouraging truths, whose importance canot be underestimated in currency matters.

The RETURN in all currencies is equal, after allowing for the cost of covering the exchange risk.

The COST of all currencies is equal, after allowing for the cost of covering the exchange risk.

For example, using the table of rates in Table A on p. xii:

	Cost of borrowing currency	Cost of cover v GBP	Total cost of GBP
	6 months % p.a.	6 months % p.a.	6 months % p.a.
GBP	$10\frac{1}{2}$	—	$10\frac{1}{2}$
DEM	$6\frac{1}{8}$	$4\frac{3}{8}$	$10\frac{1}{2}$
FRF	25	$(14\frac{1}{2})$	$10\frac{1}{2}$
NLG	$5\frac{1}{2}$	5	$10\frac{1}{2}$
ITL	26	$(15\frac{1}{2})$	$10\frac{1}{2}$
CHF	$3\frac{5}{8}$	$6\frac{7}{8}$	$10\frac{1}{2}$
etc			

2.5   Risk in Choosing Currency for the Interest Rate

Choosing a currency largely because of its interest rate is a hazardous business. We have shown examples both of borrowing a cheap currency – CHF – and of depositing a currency – NOK – because the interest rate was high. Let us tabulate the results of these two transactions.

	CHF	NOK
a: Target savings	5% p.a.	2% p.a.
b: Actual loss	12·7%*	43%
b/a Ratio	2·54 ×	21·5 ×

* calculated as $(50·37/2 - 12·5)\%$ p.a.

In Chapter 1 it was established that swings in exchange rates of the order of 20% per annum should be considered as the norm. Yet even with fairly extreme currency choices it will be rare to achieve interest rate benefits of as much as 10% per annum by switching into a different currency. This provides the basic reason why ratios of the type in the table above turn out to be so discouragingly high.

The Golden Rules to observe in this respect then are:

BORROW in a currency the company will EARN

and

DEPOSIT in a currency the company will SPEND

EXAMPLE

Given the data below,

> *a*: Which produces the cheapest Swiss francs, borrowing Swiss, or borrowing $ and doing the arbitrage?
>
> *b*: At what price can we produce $ by borrowing Swiss?

Data

Spot CHF/USD	1·8910
CHF premium, 12 months	1775 points
12 month Euro $	$15\frac{1}{16}$
12 month Euro CHF	$4\frac{1}{2}$
Period	364 days

Working

Calculation based on borrowing USD 1 million:

(i) $ required after one year @ $15\frac{1}{16}$%   1,152,299
(ii) forward CHF/USD   1·8910 − 0·1775 = 1·7135
(iii) CHF required = (i) × (ii) =   1,974,464
(iv) CHF at start, @ 1·891 =   1,891,000
(v) (iii) − (iv) =   83,464

        Equivalent to an interest rate of 4·365% p.a.

Therefore, the arbitrage is cheaper than the direct borrowing.

Calculation based on borrowing CHF 1 million:

   (i) CHF required after one year @ $4\frac{1}{2}\%$ 1,045,500

 (ii) forward CHF/USD $1\cdot8910 - 0\cdot1775 = 1\cdot7135$

(iii) USD required $= $ (i)/(ii) $=$ 610,155

(iv) USD at start, @ $1\cdot891 =$ 528,821

 (v) (iii) $-$ (iv) $=$ 81,334

       Equivalent to an interest rate of $15\cdot211\%$ p.a.

3 Invoicing in Currencies

3.1 A Facet of Marketing Policy

Companies engaged in international trade are more and more concerned with decisions about the currency in which the goods should be invoiced. Whilst trading entirely in the company's home currency has the clear advantage of simplicity, many other considerations also apply – the pros and cons have to be objectively assessed.

Exporting is, almost by definition, a market orientated business. Increasingly, the currency in which the goods are to be invoiced has become an important aspect of the overall marketing package perceived by the customer.

It should not be assumed that a company invoicing in currency need inevitably run a major foreign exchange risk. Indeed various means are available to hedge the initial currency exposure arising from export sales. The decision to invoice in currency is thus less a purely financial one, but, as we shall go on to demonstrate, more a facet of marketing policy.

3.2 Seller's 'Ideal' Currency

Other things being equal, a seller will wish to sell in his own currency. It is after all the simplest route and, if his own currency is also the currency of cost, then no exchange exposure arises requiring cover.

But in many markets buyers' preferences may well be for other currencies and insisting on, say, sterling invoicing may react adversely on sales volume. Since the effect here will be that certain sales do not materialise, such problems may be difficult to identify without on the spot investigation.

Some markets may effectively require that sales be made in the same currency as that quoted by the major competitors, which may of course not be the seller's own currency. If, for instance, a potential buyer receives four offers in dollars and one in sterling he may or may not bother to calculate whether the sterling offer is more attractive. Even if he does, he may worry as to whether the sterling offer will remain the 'best buy' *vis-à-vis* the other suppliers over the months ahead, as exchange rates fluctuate.

In a competitive market, the seller's 'ideal' currency will increasingly approximate the buyer's 'ideal' currency, which we go on to consider in more depth below. After all, the closer the seller can approximate the buyer's aims the greater chance he has to make the sale. Where the seller elects to invoice in foreign currency, usually because his prospective customers prefer it that way, then the seller should only choose one of the major currencies of the industrialised West, in which there is an active forward market for maturities at least as long as the payment period. Currencies which are of limited convertibility, chronically weak, or with only a limited forward market in London should not be considered.

Where a major export is in prospect to a country with a relatively small economy, such that the value of the contract would be a significant factor in that country's balance of payments, then additional considerations apply. The seller would be well advised to avoid any proposed contract in the buyer's currency. Particularly where the government itself, or one of its agencies, is the customer, it should be borne in mind that the customer himself is able to devalue the currency prior to payment and thus has the unusual ability to reduce the sterling or dollar cost of the goods.

3.3 Significance of the Market Leader

There are a small number of large industries where there exist clear 'Market Leaders' who dominate price setting in the industry. Such industries tend to be mature, capital intensive, and multinational. Because they are capital intensive profitability is heavily dependent upon high levels of capacity utilisation.

Consider such an industry (oil, chemicals, aluminium, etc.), where the market leader, Giant Inc., invoices into a particular market in US dollars, but a competitor, Bloggins, elects to invoice into that same market in sterling. We assume that their products are virtually indistinguishable and that both Giant Inc. and Bloggins are already running reasonably profitably, implying adequate levels of existing capacity utilisation. If sterling rises versus the dollar, Bloggins becomes uncompetitive and so its sales, capacity utilisation and profits fall. If sterling falls versus the dollar, Bloggins becomes a cheaper supplier than Giant Inc. and sales, capacity utilisation and profits rise.

But, since Bloggins was already running at fairly high capacity, it is unlikely that it can lift output as much as it would wish before it reaches some volume limitation. Bloggins will experience all of the troughs, but only a part of the peaks. The bleak arithmetic is that, on average, Bloggins must do worse than Giant Inc. And that does not take into account the undoubted production cost increases that will be caused by rapid swings in required output. Nor does it stop there.

Bloggins no doubt has many product lines, and may perhaps feel it has a particular edge in one product, Product X, having recently installed new production units with a cost advantage. Bloggins decides to promote Product X by selling it 5% cheaper than Giant Inc. sell the same items at the time. But exchange rates can and do move 5% in a single week, and by the time a salesman confronts a prospective buyer his price advantage might have disappeared or doubled. In such circumstances it is virtually impossible to carry out any coherent marketing plan, either for the business as a whole or for particular product ranges.

Perversely, even if the intended price advantage were to have doubled this may not necessarily help as much as might be thought at first sight, for the reasons set out in **3.4** below.

For all the above reasons Bloggins is likely to end up invoicing in dollars, or, more negatively, simply abandoning this market.

SELLER'S IDEAL CURRENCY
1 His currency
2 Currency stable v his currency
3 Market leader's currency
4 Currency with good forward market

3.4 Buyer's 'Ideal' Currency

For many buyers, especially in Western Europe and North America, their ideal currency will be their own currency. It has the major advantage of simplicity.

Strong buyers may be in a position to insist on their own currency being used for pricing as a condition of the deal. Quotes in other currencies will simply be ignored. This is particularly likely to be the case where a large manufacturer is buying in various minor components from abroad; it is simply not worth the trouble to get involved in foreign currency matters with 'small suppliers'.

Quotes in the buyer's currency have the advantage that they are easy to compare with quotes from other, local suppliers. This makes evaluation easier for the buyer and increases the probability that he will accept the offer, and which may also be important, do so quickly.

Smaller organisations may well prefer to be invoiced in their home currency, even at a slight price disadvantage to the foreign currency price, for the sake of 'simpler administration'.

A side advantage to the seller when selling in the buyer's currency, is that payment procedures are rendered simpler for the buyer too. All he has to do is make a payment in his own currency. It is perhaps not surprising, therefore, that payment is usually much more rapid when invoiced in the buyer's currency, typically by about two weeks. This can be a major reason for continuing to invoice in this currency, once having started to do so.

The buyer may have, or earn, currencies other than his home currency. For example, a trader in Dubai will probably have both assets and income in US dollars. In such a case the buyer will be able to accept invoicing in dollars without any currency exposure arising at all, since his income in dollars will provide a 'match' for his dollar purchases.

```
BUYER'S IDEAL CURRENCY

1  His currency
2  Currency stable v his currency
3  Currency he has
4  Currency he earns
5  Currency the others sell in
   – convenience
   – ease of justifying purchase
```

More generally, many international traders will seek to buy in the same currencies as they receive income, in order to take advantage of the opportunity to net exposure at source. This will not necessarily, or even usually, involve buying in the same currency as their home currency.

It was stated in **3.2** that some markets may effectively require that sales be made in the same currency as that quoted by the major competitors in that market, even where this is not the home currency of either the buyer or the seller. There are a number of reasons why this may be the case. Firstly, it enables comparisons to be made between competing products, thus easing the buyer's task. Fairly obvious, perhaps, but nonetheless important. Secondly, and rather more subtly, many organisations will set themselves (and their buyers) target prices for the acquisition of particular items. Such prices are likely to be set in the currency in which such goods are most usually bought, e.g.: 'Target Price USD 820/ton.'

Clearly a buyer is going to be much more confident of hitting his targets (on which his own performance will be judged) if he buys at USD 810/ton than if he buys at, say, GBP 500/ton, which may or may not work out cheaper. Even a substantial sterling discount may not seem worth the risk of prejudicing the hitting of his dollar-based target.

It can of course be argued that the buyer could take out forward cover and so lock in a fixed dollar price for his sterling priced supplies. And so he could. But many firms, and in some parts of the world such as the Middle East nearly all firms, do not do so in practice. These policies may not be capable of being altered by the buyer.

Even if the firm does accept the sterling price and cover forward to fix the dollar cost, the firm's accounting system may not allocate the dollar cost to the buyer. He may well find that he is deemed to have bought at the sterling price converted into dollars at the spot price on the accounting make up date. If so, he still cannot be sure of showing a dollar cost better than target.

3.5 Proxy Currencies

It sometimes happens that the question of the invoice currency becomes the sticking point in negotiations between buyer and seller. As we have seen, the seller's ideal currency may be very different from the buyer's. For instance, a UK importer selling to Kuwait may insist on a sterling sale, while the importer wishes to pay in Kuwaiti dinar.

The importer will be able to demonstrate that sterling has been very volatile in the past, both up and down, and that for that reason it is too risky for him to accept a sterling price. The seller could be equally determined to avoid a contract in dinar, a currency with a small and short maturity forward market, and one with which he may not be familiar. How should they resolve this dilemma?

The table below illustrates the reason for the Kuwaiti's understandable concern, and also a possible compromise solution.

Currency Swings, % movement during 1981		
Currency	v USD	v GBP
Saudi Arabia	4	25
Canada	5	25
Kuwait	6	23
South Africa	25	10
Nigeria	24	6

Setting the price in dollars will reduce the Kuwaiti's risk from a typical 23% of the price down to something more like 6%, or by a factor of around four. From the seller's point of view there is no problem in covering his dollar receivables into sterling using the foreign exchange market.

More comprehensive tables of this type can easily be constructed. Any firm selling into a number of markets overseas would be well advised to construct its own, listing all its markets and showing the volatility of each buyer's home currency against at least USD, GBP, DEM, and JPY.

The table above makes it clear why UK firms who export only in sterling are so successful in markets like Africa, and also why they do less well in, say, the Middle East. Conversely, dollar pricing exporters may do well in the Middle East, less well in Africa. The message is that different currencies are likely to be optimal in different markets.

This use of a 'proxy currency', i.e. the choice of a currency likely to behave similarly to the buyer's currency, is a frequently used method of resolving the buyer/seller dilemma. Another technique, at one time very widespread but nowadays falling into disuse, is the Currency Clause price whereby payment is made in one currency but the amount due is fixed by reference to another. This method, which acts as a proxy currency at one remove, has no obvious advantages over straight proxy currency invoicing and is not recommended.

3.6 Currency Conversion Costs

In every export contract someone does a foreign exchange transaction. It may be the exporter if he is selling in currency; it may be the importer if he is buying in a currency other than his own. If the currency of the contract is not the home currency for either importer or exporter then both will have to do a foreign exchange transaction. It seems sensible to arrange matters between exporter and importer so that the cost of doing the foreign exchange contracts shall be minimised.

For minor currencies it is usually the case that the only real market is in the country of the currency itself. Currencies like the Irish pound and the Nigerian naira, although traded in London, will be more economically handled within those countries. The overall cost of conducting the trade will therefore be minimised by selling into those countries in a major currency and leaving it to the importer to buy the necessary funds locally.

Foreign exchange markets within Europe vary widely in their competitiveness and commission structure for handling corporate foreign exchange business. As an example, owing to Exchange Control regulations in France, a French company must do its foreign exchange transactions with a bank within France. Commissions are high by UK standards, but the company has no opportunity to deal in the cheaper London market. The same is true in the Scandinavian countries, but to a greater extent since the very small number of local banks available to the corporate dealer results in even less competition.

Wherever one of the parties to the trade is in a country where exchange transactions are relatively expensive it may be worth considering changing the currency so that the FX deals may be handled more economically. This is obviously of particular relevance in respect of intra-group trading. That is, for the Anglo-French trade invoice in French francs so that no transaction arises in France and the GBP/FRF transaction can be done in London.

Where sales into a particular country are routed through an agent and the currency of the trade is foreign to him the agent may well build in 'allowances' into his selling prices to cover himself against the risk he runs. These 'allowances' may far exceed the actual cost of cover in the London FX market and are sometimes quite randomly arrived at. The result is that the goods become dearer to the end buyer than they need be, and sales volume will suffer.

3.7   Setting Equivalent Price in Currency

There is a hidden trap in setting prices in foreign currency. It is of the simplest kind, so much so that some very sophisticated treasurers fall into it every time. Suppose a company produces a product for export which it would normally sell at, say, GBP 100,000, but elects for marketing reasons to price the product in Swiss francs. The spot rate of exchange is, say 3·2650 Swiss francs to the pound. What more natural to suppose the price should be:

100,000 × 3·2650 = CHF 326,500?

However, some pause for thought is necessary at this point. The exchange rate above is good for Swiss francs received value spot, i.e. two days from now, and for conversion to sterling then. But payment in two days' time is extremely unlikely; it is almost certain that payment will be made on the usual terms of the trade, perhaps six months hence. Now, bearing in mind that had the firm invoiced in sterling it would have received GBP 100,000 six months hence, what is required is the exchange rate that will similarly produce GBP 100,000 six months hence by conversion of the Swiss francs on that date.

It follows that the exchange rate required for converting the sterling price to currency is the outright price for the expected date of payment, here the six month outright price. If this is done and forward contracts taken out immediately, the sterling cash flow will be precisely the same irrespective of the change in the invoice currency. For this reason it can be argued that the decision as to the correct currency for invoicing is purely a marketing matter, since there is no effect on the cash flow at all. It is tempting for the financial function to enquire why this marketing aspect is so vital, seeing that the cash flow turns out the same either way. But the point is that although the cash flow is identical per transaction, the marketing group will no doubt assert that they will get more transactions done. The benefit arises from the improvement in sales volume.

A further example of the arithmetic involved is set out overleaf, this time using the case of the Italian lira.

Equivalent Currency Price

    a: Breakeven price in GBP 400,000
All costs in sterling
Payment due in 6 months

    b: What must we charge in lira to at least achieve our breakeven return?

    c: Lira exchange rates v GBP are:
Spot   2400
6 months 2490

    d: The price that yields GBP 400,000 in 6 months is:
400,000 × 2490 = Lira 996 million
NOT   400,000 × 2400 = Lira 960 million

    e: The company can now sell the Lira 996 million to yield GBP 400,000 at existing forward exchange rates.

3.8   Longer Term Strategies

None of the above many reasons for settling for a particular currency were specifically interested in the question of whether the selected currency was expected to be weak or strong. It was assumed that the currency risk would be covered in any case so that the company would not experience any gain or loss in the event of a currency movement.

All of the arguments were concerned with the marketing aspect. Some companies, however, seek to invoice only in 'strong' currencies and devote their time and effort to altering their invoicing currency whenever their perception of currency outlook alters. In countries without Exchange Control this is wasted effort, since if the company wishes to be long of particular currencies it is free to go and buy them whether or not there is any underlying trade. This more direct method of position taking has the advantage of being rapidly adjustable without deleterious effects on the company's basic business and customer relationships.

Despite the above, there are certain circumstances where a currency may logically be chosen as the invoicing currency precisely because it is expected to be either strong or weak, as the case may be. The most common such reason is to be able to maintain stable price lists in industries where new price lists are expensive to alter and therefore infrequently issued.

Longer term objectives may also be pursued by means of an appropriate choice of invoice currency. For instance, the currency of invoicing may be selected to enable 'invisible' price changes to be made, perhaps to protect market share for short periods in line with some longer term objective. That is, a company having a substantial market share in a country expected to have a weak market for its products in the short term, may decide to invoice in a currency expected to be similarly weak. As the currency depreciates, the customer will receive an increasing discount on the goods without the company ever having to announce a price reduction. Thus market share can be protected (at a cost) until business conditions improve.

Similarly, a company in a strong position may well be able to specify a very strong currency as its invoicing currency, thus reaping the benefit of a continuously rising return via currency appreciation, without actually having to negotiate any formal price increase.

SELF TEST QUESTIONS

Answer the following questions using, where appropriate, the data given in the Table A on page xii.

1 An exporter selling to North Africa proposes to sell in USD. His costs are wholly in GBP and the lowest acceptable price on the transaction is GBP 156,000. If payment is in three months what is the equivalent price in dollars?

2 In the above example the customer makes a counter offer of FRF 1.7 million. Is this acceptable?

Answers
1 3 month USD/GBP = 1·62725 − 0·0047 = 1·62255
  USD price = GBP 156,000 × 1·62255 = USD 253,118

2 Equivalent price in FRF is given by a similar calculation:
  3 month FRF/USD = 6·67625 + 0·30375 = 6·98
  FRF price = 253,118 × 6·98 = FRF 1,766,764
  So an offer of FRF 1·7 million is not acceptable.

Note that in this example use of the spot rate for the calculation would produce a FRF price of only FRF 1,694,773, which would falsely suggest that 1·7 million is 'about right'. But this price would give rise to a loss in sterling when covered forward.

4 Covering Currency Risk

4.1 Forward Contract

Forward contracts are the normal means of achieving foreign exchange risk cover. The classic case is perhaps an exporter of say, furniture which, for marketing reasons, is to be priced in US dollars. Let us suppose the shipment is to be paid for on 18 September, and that the amount due is $251,102·00. The exporter would normally take out a forward contract to sell the dollar proceeds and buy sterling for settlement on 18 September at an exchange rate agreed today. This then fixes the sterling value of his sale and renders him indifferent to any market fluctuations in the dollar/sterling exchange rate thereafter.

In the meantime his dollar asset of the receivable is precisely cancelled out (from the currency risk point of view) by the dollar liability of the forward contract; both will extinguish simultaneously on the due date of 18 September. This situation is illustrated in the diagram 'Single Receipt on Known Date'.

So far, so good. What has been established is that forward contracts provide a simple and economic method of cover when the currency cash flow is reasonably accurately known. But financial and administrative costs may mount up if the company frequently seeks earlier or later settlement than the due date for the forward.

SINGLE RECEIPT ON KNOWN DATE.
Covered by foreign currency forward contract

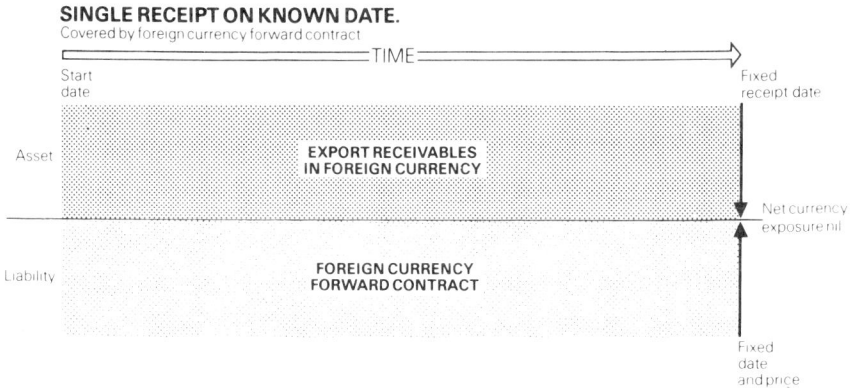

4.2   **Option Date Forward Contract**

A standard foreign exchange contract is for settlement on an agreed, fixed date. The option date forward contract extends this idea to allow the customer to call for settlement of the contract on two days' notice at any time in an 'option period' agreed with the bank on the day the deal was struck. Thus a company may agree to sell dollars and buy sterling for settlement on any date between 18 August and 20 October and the bank will quote one rate good for settlement at any time within this option period.

It is entirely up to the company to choose the two dates to suit the likely pattern of their payments and receipts. The closer together the two dates are – that is the shorter the option period – the finer price the bank will be able to make. (This is because the customer now has the right to call at any date in the period and the bank will assume that the call will be made on the date most expensive to the bank and will price the option date contract accordingly. The most expensive date is usually the first or last date of the option period.) The option applies only to the settlement date; settlement must be made at some time during the option period, at latest on the last day.

In many industries there is always uncertainty to some extent as to the exact payment dates, even though the amounts due may be relatively easily ascertained and few in number. Whenever the amounts due are relatively few and are known in amount, but where there is some latitude in the payment date, option date contracts are a useful solution. Referring to the diagram 'Single Receipt on Uncertain Date' it will be seen that the option feature enables the

SINGLE RECEIPT ON UNCERTAIN DATE.
Covered by foreign currency forward contract with option

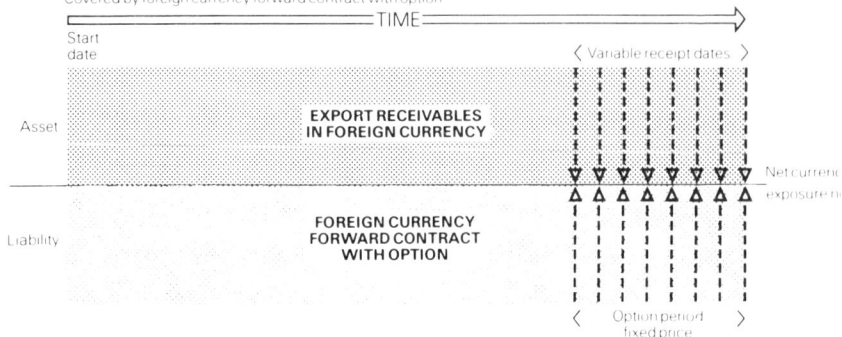

TIME

Start
date
⟨ Variable receipt dates ⟩

Asset

**EXPORT RECEIVABLES
IN FOREIGN CURRENCY**

Net current
exposure n

Liability

**FOREIGN CURRENCY
FORWARD CONTRACT
WITH OPTION**

⟨ Option period
fixed price ⟩

maturity date on the forward contract to adjust to match the payment date and keep the net currency risk to zero.

The disadvantages of option date forward contracts are that they can be relatively expensive if the option periods cannot be kept short and that they become unwieldy to administer if the number of individual payments and payment dates becomes large.

4.3   Currency Overdraft

Borrowing the currency concerned is an alternative to covering the currency risk in the foreign exchange market and is an economical solution where the cash flow consists of a large number of individual items, especially where dates of payment are uncertain.

The principle is that the customer borrows an amount of currency that exactly matches his receivables in amount. The currency borrowed is immediately sold for sterling and the sterling used to reduce the company's existing sterling debt, if any. Total borrowing and balance sheet ratios are now precisely the same as before of course, but the make up by currency has altered. Each currency receipt is used to part repay the loan so that the currency receivable will continue to match the currency liability (the loan) irrespective of the amounts or payment dates of individual receipts. Exchange risk is therefore exactly matched whatever the cash flow pattern. This is shown on the diagram, 'Numerous Receipts on Uncertain Dates'.

If the currency overdraft is used to replace a domestic overdraft little if any additional cost will arise, but if the company is not in a

NUMEROUS RECEIPTS ON UNCERTAIN DATES.
Covered by foreign currency overdraft

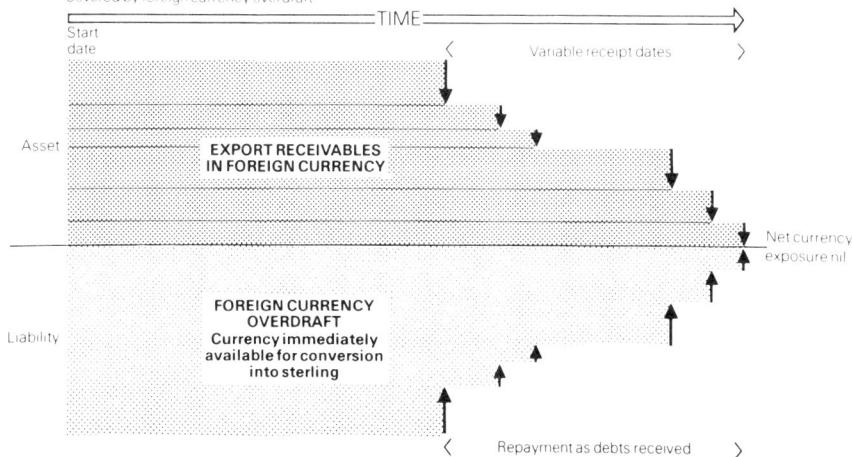

borrowing position the banker's margin will become an additional cost and will cause the method to become less attractive.

4.4   Multicurrency Cash Flows

Revenue in a large number of currencies may be covered on an approximate basis by using overdrafts in relatively few currencies. Since many currencies tend to follow a dominant currency in their group (e.g. Canadian $ follows US $ more closely than say the DEM does), it is possible to use an overdraft currency per group and so simplify the problem.

The table 'Currency Overdrafts' on p. 32 shows an example of this type of arrangement. Use of a greater number of currencies (if there is a market for them) will improve the accuracy of cover, but will increase complexity and admin costs. The 'best' balance is up to the treasurer to decide.

4.5   Overdrafts in Practice

In practice, overdrafts and receivables do not just wind down to zero as portrayed in the 'Currency Exposure on Exports' diagrams (pp. 29, 30 and 31); new sales are constantly being invoiced out. There

CURRENCY OVERDRAFTS

Receivables	Exchange rate/$	Advance in $
$2,106,481	1	2,106,481
Saudi 1,813,206	3·40	533,295
		$2,639,776
	Convert to £ @ 1.75 = £1,508,443	
	& credit to £ account	

Receivables	Exchange rate/DM	Advance in DM
DM 710,000	1	710,000
Dfl 1,412,300	0·91	1,285,193
SK 1,046,000	0·40	418,400
		DM2,413,593
	Convert to £ @ 4.29 = £562,609	
	& credit to £ account	

must therefore be some mechanism to maintain the overdraft balance in line with the receivables on a rolling basis.

The simplest, and most widely used method is illustrated in the diagram 'Currency Overdrafts – Case 1' (p. 33). Here the currency inflow is sold spot for sterling on receipt and so does not alter the level of the currency overdraft, which appears as a horizontal line. This is equivalent to an assumption that that receivables book will remain constant over time. At regular intervals the account balance is checked against the receivables book and small net drawdowns or repayments made to restore parity.

The method above has deficiencies from a lending banker's point of view in that the banker is looking to the income to secure the loan (whether formally or informally). There are two problems:

a: the income is not used to pay down the loan, so violating the 'self liquidating transaction' criterion;

b: the loan may exceed the receivables by uncontrolled and variable amounts.

CURRENCY OVERDRAFTS

1:Overdraft balance may exceed
  receivables, cash flow not used
  to pay down loans

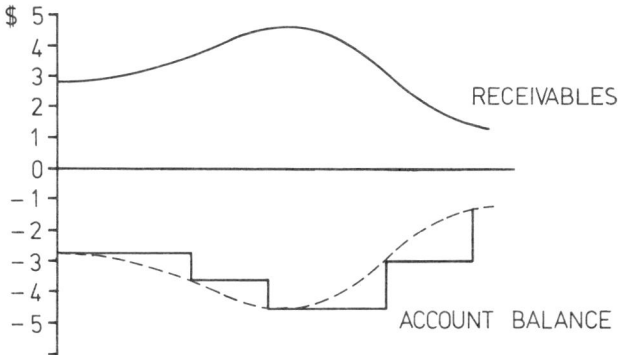

-Cash flow sold spot on receipt
-Balance is adjusted to equal current
  receivables from time to time

AVERAGE NET EXPOSURE ZERO
          (but with built-in lag)

The second diagram, 'Currency Overdrafts – Case 2' (p. 35), illustrates a means of avoiding these problems. The first problem is met by simply requiring that all the relevant currency income is applied in reduction of the loan. Since this will cause the loan balance to continually fall, the second ingredient is a regular top-up mechanism. The company draws down a fixed tranche size, say $T, every time it finds the loan balance has fallen to an amount $\frac{1}{2}$T below receivables. It is not permitted to draw down more than the actual receivables plus $\frac{1}{2}$T.

Thus the balance will fluctuate $\frac{1}{2}$T either side of the actual receivables and, on average, the position will be in balance. Yet the bank will now be able to control its level of risk.

The third diagram (p. 36) shows a more complex technique, used only rarely, where a bank is unwilling to see any unsecured element in the loan at all. As will be seen, the overdraft top-up works in the same way as above but the loan account balance is always $\frac{1}{2}$T lower than before. The resultant net exposure of $\frac{1}{2}$T is covered by a forward contract of $\frac{1}{2}$T, which is replaced on each expiry so that there is always one such contract in place.

This last method is clumsy, but it does serve to introduce the idea of using forward contracts in combination with loan accounts in various ways to provide economical and convenient cover. For instance:

a: Take out forward contracts to the first likely payment date (near date) and then handle later payment by means of a currency overdraft.

b: Use a fixed currency loan to the near date and then handle later payment by means of a currency overdraft.

c: Take out forward contracts to the far date; if paid earlier, deposit the currency until required to meet the forward contract.

Some of these techniques are illustrated in the example in **4.6** below.

4.6   Relative Economics

An example with real numbers will perhaps illustrate the issues more clearly.

CURRENCY OVERDRAFTS

2: Averaging technique if overdraft
   balance may exceed receivables,
   but receivables must be used to
   pay down overdraft

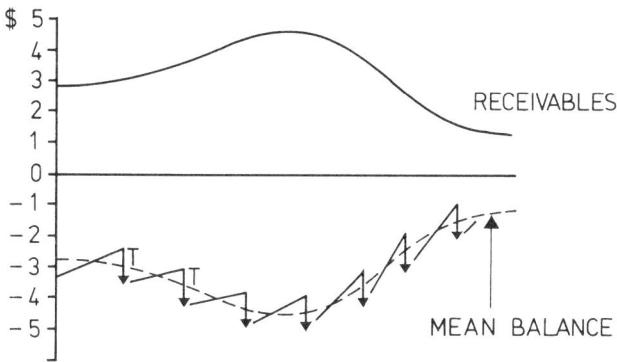

Receivables level	= $ R
Tranche size	= $ T
Initial drawing	= R+½T
Trigger Level for new tranche	= R−½T
Mean balance	= R

AVERAGE NET EXPOSURE ZERO

CURRENCY OVERDRAFTS

3: Averaging technique if overdraft
   balance may NOT exceed receivables

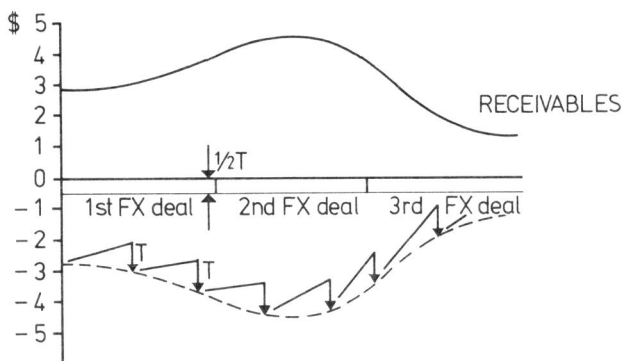

Receivables	$= \$R$
Tranche size	$= \$T$
Initial drawing	$= R$
Trigger Level for new tranche	$= R-T$
Mean balance	$= R-\tfrac{1}{2}T$
Forward cover	$= \tfrac{1}{2}T$

AVERAGE NET EXPOSURE ZERO

Situation

Bloggins Ltd is due to receive $750,000 some time in July, but cannot be sure exactly when. Bloggins has substantial net borrowings on sterling overdraft at 1% over Base Rate, which on 4 January 1983 stands at 10%. The company also has available a currency facility allowing either overdrafts or drawings for fixed periods at $\frac{3}{4}$% over current overdraft rate or market lending rate for the fixed periods. Company policy is to cover exchange risks. Rate information is otherwise as given in Table A on p. xii.

Solution 1

Cover by fixed date forward contract taken out to the beginning of July, then extended as necessary until receipt of the funds. Finance the receivable by continued drawdown on the sterling overdraft.

Cost of finance @ 1 over Base Rate $= 11\%$
Gain on forward contract premium $= 10\frac{1}{2} - 9\frac{5}{16} = 1\frac{3}{16}\%$
Net cost of finance $= 11 - 1\frac{3}{16} = 9\frac{13}{16}\%$ p.a.

Risks

a: Sterling Base Rate may go up. (It did, by 1%, as soon as 12 January 1983!)

b: The 'extra' forward premium we assume we will receive for the part month of July may be lower, nil, or negative by the time we reach July.

Solution 2

Use an option date forward contract. An option date forward contract price is based on either the 'near' date or the 'far' date depending on which is dearer. The dearer date here is the near date, since the company will receive least premium on that date. Consequently the option period should be chosen to get the near date as distant as possible. Note that an option 'to end July' would be priced at the spot rate, i.e. 1·6275, whereas an option for 'the month of July' would be priced at the six month outright price, i.e. approximately 1·6185, since in the first case the near date is spot, in the second case six months away.

Assuming a contract is taken out 'for the month of July' then the economics will be the same as *Solution 1* except that the risk in (*b*) is eliminated along with all possibility of receipt of any further premium for the part month of July. Cost is therefore:

Until 1 July $= 9\frac{13}{16}$ (strictly Base Rate $- \frac{3}{16}$)
Thereafter   Base Rate $+ 1$

Solution 3
Use a currency overdraft. Cost here is simple to calculate as $ overdraft rate, $9\frac{1}{8}\%$, plus the markup of $\frac{3}{4}\% = 9\frac{7}{8}\%$.

Risk
$ overdraft rate may go up.

Solution 4
Use a currency loan. Fixed loans for six months in dollars are available at $9\frac{5}{16} + \frac{3}{4} = 10\frac{1}{16}\%$.

This obviates the risk in *Solution 3* but also means that no benefit will be derived from any subsequent falls in dollar interest rates. Cover by overdraft will be required from the six month date until the funds actually arrive and extinguish the liability. The risk in this phase is the same as in *Solution 3* above.

4.7 Tenders in Currency

Here is one of the thorniest problems in limiting currency risk. Typically, an exporter is asked to tender in currency for a contract overseas. He must give a firm price, but the exchange rate can change between the date of his submission and the date the tender is accepted. Yet he cannot cover his forward risk, because he cannot be sure he will get the contract. (Indeed, on a statistical basis he will probably fail to get a majority of the jobs he tenders for, perhaps winning only one in four: the rub is he doesn't know which one of the four it is, otherwise he would never submit a losing tender.) The problem is compounded by the very nature of the type of job that gives rise to a tender. The job is very large relative to the firm's turnover and net worth; it may represent a relatively long term commitment to a project, and by definition it is likely to be very competitively priced. In a word, the firm cannot afford to get it wrong. So what can the firm do to limit the risks to an acceptable level?

There are a number of possible routes. Some of them may be ruled out in a particular situation, but none should not be tried simply because someone thinks the customer won't wear it. Certainly a tenderer is constrained to quote under the terms of the tender, but he is not forbidden to offer other alternatives to the buyer if he wishes, available in addition to the main, conforming tender. Possible methods are:

a: Quote in the currency of cost. This may comprise a number of currencies, including for many projects a considerable element of the customer's local currency. For instance, a construction project in Saudi Arabia would no doubt involve considerable local expense in Saudi riyals for earthmoving and other local content. It would be surprising if the customer were resistant to having part of the quote in his own currency, which after all eliminates currency risk for both parties.

b: If the job is principally exporting items manufactured in the UK but to be priced in dollars the situation is a little more stark. But try using a currency clause so that the dollar price moves according to the dollar/sterling rate at the time of acceptance. This is bypassing the matter, quoting in dollars but securing a fixed sterling price nonetheless.

c: Build in a cushion into the pricing to allow for the likely movement in the currency of tender during the tender period. Use of the tables shown in **1.1** (p. 2, or others like it that the treasurer can construct for himself based on the actual movements experienced over the recent past) provides a means of quantifying the size of the cushion required. The one sure fact is that the sales department will not believe the cushion needs to be this large and will be very concerned about the chances of getting the order on this basis. The treasurer's problem at this time is to be able to justify his figures, and to point out the hazards of actually getting the order at the wrong price as opposed to the more obvious problems of not getting the order.

d: Since the size of the cushion depends directly on the length of the tender period, consider trying to negotiate that the tender period be reduced, e.g. from six months to three.

Perhaps the best way to illustrate the issues involved is with a concrete example.

EXAMPLE

A British contractor is required to tender for an overseas construction project in US dollars. He requires a price of GBP 10 million to meet his UK costs and target margin. At the date of the tender the spot rate is 1·5380. The tender has a 3 month validity. Assume forward premia are at par (zero). What price can he quote, assuming:

a: he must quote a fixed US dollar price, or

b: he can offer a price clause alternative. What will the formula be in the price clause? What will the dollar price be if the spot exchange rate is 1·60 on the signature date?

c: Let us now further assume that, after the 3 month period is over rates have moved to:

spot   1·6864
1 year   1·6920
2 years   1·7020
3 years   1·7050
4 years   1·7110
5 years   1·7200

Assume the contract terms are for equal payments to be made on signature and on each of the 5 anniversaries, $\frac{1}{6}$ on each date. If we get the order and cover forward immediately we do so, what are the sterling proceeds under the two different quotation methods above?

d: Why have we still ended up with proceeds below the intended GBP 10 million?

e: How could we have sought to prevent this?

Solution

a: Dollar price is $10,000,000 \times 1·5380 \times 1·1$

$$= \$16,918,000.$$

(10% fluctuation likely in 3 months according to the table in **1.1**)

b: On the second basis, the formula price is initially $10,000,000 \times 1·5380$

$$= \$15,380,000.$$

But the price is to be modified according to a price clause formula of the form:

$ price = $15,380,000 × spot rate on signature/1·5380

Therefore, if the spot price on signature is 1·6000, then the dollar price is given by:

$15,380,000 × 1·6000/1·5380

$$= $16,000,000.$$

c: The quoted price was $16,918,000. the average forward price at which cover can now be obtained is the average outright price for the six payment dates:

(1·6864 + 1·6920 + 1·7020 + 1·7050 + 1·7110 + 1·7200)/6

$$= 1·702733$$

Sterling proceeds will be $16,918,000/1·702733

$$= GBP 9,935,791.$$

On the formula basis, at a spot rate of 1·6864 the quote becomes $16,864,000.

Converted at the outright rate of 1·702733 this converts to GBP 16,864,000/1·702733

$$= GBP 9,904,078.$$

d: Although the company estimated that the spot price would move up to 10% in the 3 months, and even though it in fact moved less than this (1·5380 to 1·6864 is 9·6%), there was a net loss because the forward premium moved. The difference in the formula case was entirely due to this shift in the premium.

e: It would be possible to allow for possible swings in the premium either by building in a larger cushion into the fixed price alternative, or by using a forward outright price rather than a spot price in the formula basis. Commercial reality normally makes this refinement, however desirable, uncompetitive.

All the above expensive dilemmas highlight the business requirement for a means of cover that is totally effective in a situation where the cash flow to be covered is not yet a commercial fact. The tender is the classic case, but an international takeover shares the same characteristics; if we get the deal then we need cover, but we don't know yet if we will get the deal, so we dare not cover.

It is precisely this situation that can be best handled by the new markets in currency options. These we turn to next.

1 Using rates from Table A in p. xii, calculate the price a company would pay for an option date forward contract HKD/GBP from spot to the three month date.

    a: to buy HKD against sterling

    b: to sell HKD against sterling

2 Some companies only borrow on currency overdraft if the interest rate is below sterling overdraft rates. Is this a reasonable policy?

3 In **4.6** what should Bloggins do?

Answers

1

	spot	premium	outright
HKD/USD	6·5120/70	70/20	6·5050/5150
USD/GBP	1·6270/75	49/44	1·6221/30
HKD/GBP	10.5950/10·6064		10·5518/10·5738

    a: Company buys HKD, option spot to 3 months priced on the far date, @ 10·5518.

    b: Company sells HKD, option spot to 3 months priced on the near date, @ 10·6064.

2 No. This is the 'interest rate trap' again. Refer back to **2.3** (p. 11).

3 Readers are here free to weigh up for themselves the pros and cons of each course of action as it seems at the outset of the problem. The 'best' solution will rely entirely on a correct guess as to the course of future interest rates in sterling and dollars in the period January to July. The purpose of this example is to make the reader aware that covering the exchange risk is only achieved by the assumption of another, lesser, risk – that of a shift in interest rates.

5 Economics of Currency Options

5.1   Nature of an Option Contract

A true currency option gives the holder the right to buy (or sell) a currency at a given price but creates no obligation to do so. These true options are different in kind from option date forward contracts which provide an option only as to the date when exchange shall take place, but require exchange at some time within the option period. The difference has been aptly summarised as 'whether to' options as opposed to 'when to' options.

Some currency option business takes place through specialist options exchanges where standard contracts are traded having specified contract amounts, delivery dates and other parameters. Many commercial banks also deal in currency options for their clients.

There are two parties to a currency option contract, the buyer and the seller, or 'writer'. The option buyer pays a premium to the option seller and in return receives a commitment to exchange the contract amount of foreign currency at the agreed price at any time until the expiry date of the option. The exchange rate at which the deal is struck is called the 'strike price' or 'exercise price'. Whereas the buyer has the right to demand purchase or sale of the currency concerned, unlike all other currency markets he has no obligation to do so. He may exercise his option or not, as he chooses. He thus has a true option to exchange currency at the strike price. Seen from the point of view of the buyer, if rates move in his favour he can exercise the option and take the gain; if rates move against him he will not exercise the option and cannot experience a loss greater than the premium he paid at the outset.

The seller of the option on the other hand, by accepting the premium also accepts the obligation to exchange the specified currency at the strike price on demand from the buyer, no matter what the exchange rate is at the time, so that his possible risk is unlimited.

5.2   The Call and the Put

A call option gives the holder the right to buy a currency (against delivery of US dollars). The buyer of a call thus expects the currency concerned to strengthen *vis-à-vis* the dollar. The economics of options are conventionally illustrated by means of an options profit chart of the type shown for a call option. The chart shows profit or loss on the vertical scale and exchange rate along the horizontal scale, and so shows how the profit outturn will vary with exchange rate. As

PROFIT CHART - BUYING A CALL OPTION

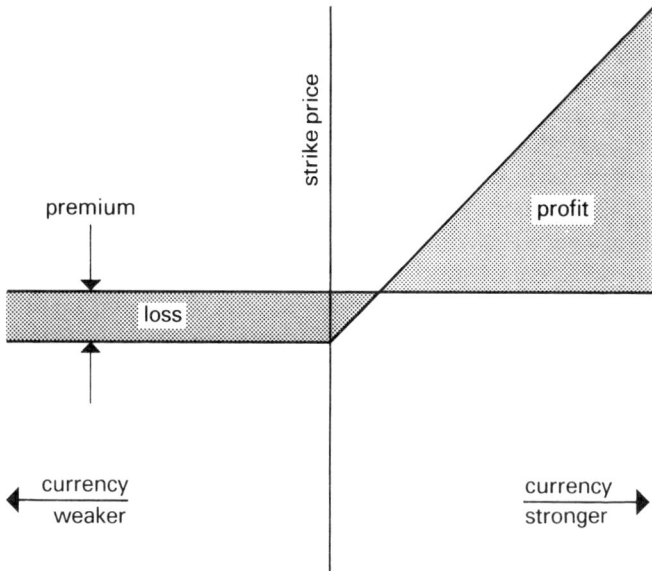

premium

strike price

profit

loss

currency weaker

currency stronger

can be seen from the chart, if the exchange rate at a given moment in the option period is at or below the strike price, exercise of the option would not occur, as to do so would incur a loss, and the option buyer's loss is equal to the premium he paid. If the exchange rate rises above the strike price then the option would be exercised, and the greater the rise in the currency the greater the proceeds. If the proceeds exceed the premium paid, then the call buyer has a profit. The key point is that, unlike most other financial instruments, options are not symmetric. With an option, the buyer is under no obligation to exercise an option at a loss, so his 'worst case' is the cost of the premium. He has LIMITED LOSS potential but UNLIMITED PROFIT potential.

In the next diagram the profit chart for the call buyer is repeated along with those for the other three possible transactions: buying a put, selling a call, and selling a put. It will be seen from the second of

1. Buy Call

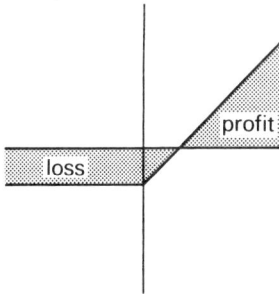

2. Buy Put

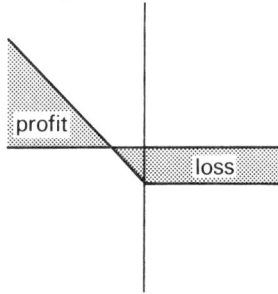

3. Sell Call

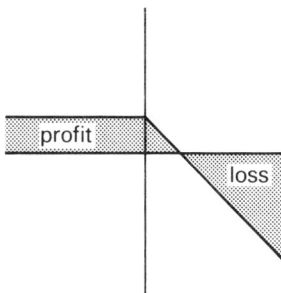

4. Sell Put

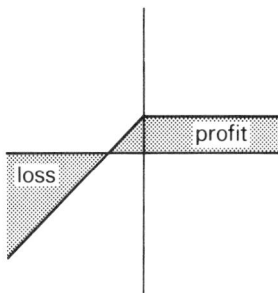

these charts that, as might be expected, the buyer of a put is in a similar position to that of the call buyer save that he has a right to sell the currency *vis-à-vis* the dollar, and will profit if the currency weakens against the dollar. Again, his maximum loss is limited to the premium he paid.

The picture is precisely reversed for option sellers as is shown in the second two charts. The writer must pitch the level of the premium he charges so as to compensate him for the likely incidence of options being exercised by buyers with a profit. The seller has LIMITED PROFIT potential and UNLIMITED LOSS potential.

5.3 Philadelphia Market Specifications

A number of markets exist which trade in currency options. These include the options exchanges of Amsterdam, Montreal, Vancouver and Philadelphia, and may over the next few years come to include futures exchanges such as the IMM in Chicago and LIFFE in London (London International Financial Futures Exchange – pronounced as 'life') who may offer option contracts alongside or in conjunction with their existing currency futures contracts. Further, a number of banks, in New York, London and on the continent of Europe, offer various types of service in options, sometimes of a 'tailor made' nature for particular customers. Amongst the exchanges which are offering a service in currency options, the principal market thus far is the Philadelphia Stock Exchange. For this reason, although most of the following material will be valid for options generally, specific examples will use the contract specifications and quotation conventions of the Philadelphia market.

The Philadelphia Stock Exchange operates a market for currency options in five currencies:

- Deutsche marks
- Swiss francs
- Canadian dollars
- British pounds
- Japanese yen

The contract sizes have in each case been set equal to one half of the equivalent currency futures contracts traded on the IMM in Chicago in order to encourage arbitrage business between the two markets.

CONTRACT SPECIFICATIONS

	Deutsche marks	Swiss francs	Canadian dollars	British pounds	Japanese yen
Underlying Currency Units	62,500	62,500	50,000	12,500	6,250,000
Exercise Price Intervals	2¢	2¢	2¢	5¢	.02¢
Exercise Price and Premium Quotations	Cents/Unit	Cents/Unit	Cents/Unit	Cents/Unit	Hundredths Cents/Unit
Minimum Premium Change	·01	·01	·01	·05	·01
Minimum Contract Price Change	$6·25	$6·25	$5·00	$6·25	$6·25
Expiration Months	March, June, September and December				
Expiration Cycles	3, 6 and 9 months				
Expiration Date	Saturday before the third Wednesday of the month				
Expiration Settlement Date	Third Wednesday of the month				
Delivery Method	Foreign Currency Purchaser: Delivers dollars thru clearing member to OCC bank account				
	Foreign Currency Seller: Delivers currency to OCC account in the country of currency				
Issuer & Guarantor	Options Clearing Corporation (OCC)				
Margin for Uncovered Writer	At or in the money: 130% of premium + $750 (maximum margin is premium plus $2500)				
	Out of the money: 130% of premium + $750 less out of the money amount (minimum margin is 130% of premium + $250)				
Trading Hours:	8:30 A.M. to 2:30 P.M. EST				
Position and Exercise Units:	10,000 Contracts				

Courtesy of The Philadelphia Stock Exchange Inc.

Exchange rates, including strike prices, are quoted in US terms, that is in US cents per unit of currency. In the case of the Japanese yen prices are quoted as US cents per 100 units of currency. The table below shows the conventional foreign exchange market quotation versus the Philadelphia market convention.

Exchange Rate Quotation Conventions		
Currency	FX market quote	Phila quote
Sterling	1·55	155
Deutsche mark	2·50	40
Swiss franc	2·2222	45
Can dollar	0·8128	81·28
Japanese yen	246.18	40·62*

* US cents/100 yen

The market trades contracts for standard strike prices; strike prices are always round numbers and the interval between them is part of the contract specification. At any given time the market will trade for three strike prices, being:

- the strike price closest to the cash foreign exchange market
- one price interval higher than this
- one price interval lower than this

For example, supposing marks were trading in the spot market at 1 DM = $0·3863, then Philadelphia would be offering options contracts at three strike prices: at 38 being the closest to spot, 40 being one interval up and 36 being one interval down. (Referring to the table of contract specifications on page 47 it will be seen that, for the Deutsche mark, exercise prices are quoted in even numbers of cents per mark, and the exercise price interval is two cents.)

Premium is priced in points per Deutsche mark (one point is 1/100 of one US cent) and quoted to the nearest point. If the premium changes by this one point minimum then the cost of the contract changes by $6·25 per contract. This $6·25 is also the same for the other currencies, except for the Canadian dollar, where it is $5 per contract.

Currency option contracts are traded for standard delivery dates; expiration months are March, June, September and December. At any given date the next three of these are traded. The expiration date, which is the last time that an option may be exercised, is set as the Saturday before the third Wednesday of the month concerned, with settlement occurring on that third Wednesday. Individual banks and brokers who deal on behalf of customers on the exchange would normally require final notice well before the exchanges' Saturday deadline.

Margin

Buyers of call or put options do not have to concern themselves with margin. They simply pay their premium and unless and until they close out their deal they have no other payments in or out.

By contrast an option writer has further responsibilities to the exchange in respect of margin. This arises because the writer is required to meet any option if called and so has unlimited risk. The way in which the exchange ensures that the writer is always in a position to meet his commitments is by requiring writers to put up cash deposits or some other type of margin acceptable to the exchange in respect of the business written. The scale of this margin is set by the exchange and is defined according to whether the contract currently is in-the-money (that is, would provide the buyer with a profit if exercised) or out-of-the-money. The scale of margin required from writers is as below.

Margin requirements for writers are set according to rules which at first appear somewhat complex. Margin per contract, M, is given by:

$$M = 1{\cdot}3 \times \text{premium} + Z$$

where $Z = \$750 -$ out of the money amount, if any, or
$\$250$, whichever the greater.

Also, there is an upper limit on margin, given by:

$$\text{max}\,M = \text{premium} + \$2500$$

This upper limit only comes into effect if the premium per contract is in excess of \$5750.

Examples of Margin Calculation

  (i) DM contract, premium \$1500 per contract, currently in the money.
  $Z = \$750 - \text{nil} = \$750$
  $M = 1{\cdot}3 \times 1500 + 750 = \$2700$
  $\text{max}\,M = 1500 + 2500 = \$4000$, i.e. not applicable.
  Margin required is \$2700.

(ii) Premium is $1000 per contract, out of the money by 91 points. One point is worth $6·25, so the out of the money amount is $6·25 × 91 = $568·75.
$Z = 750 - 568·75 = $181·25$, but this is below $250, so that Z becomes $250
$M = 1·3 × 1000 + 250 = 1550
$maxM = 1000 + 2500 = 3500, not applicable
Margin required is $1550

(iii) Contract is in the money and premium is $6000 per contract.
$Z = 750 - nil = 750
$M = 1·3 × 6000 + 750 = 8550
$maxM = 6000 + 2500 = 8500
Margin required is $8500.

Margin may be waived for so-called 'covered writers' who can demonstrate that they hold the underlying currency available for delivery against possible exercise of the option, US dollars in the case of put writers and the contract currency in the case of call writers. In turn this must be evidenced by:

a: funds transferred to a bank designated by the options broker or bank handling the business, or

b: 'option guarantee letter' from a bank holding the funds, which undertakes to deliver the funds to the broker against countervalue at the exercise price if called upon to do so, or

c: banker's letter of credit, undertaking to pay the requisite amount on demand.

5.4 Intrinsic Value and Time Value

The premia for currency options are dependent upon three principal factors:

a: the difference between the exercise price and the current spot price

b: the time until expiry of the option

c: the volatility of the exchange rate concerned

An option premium is normally thought of as consisting of two components, intrinsic value and time value. The intrinsic value is simply the profit difference, if any, between the existing spot price and the exercise price. That is, for a call option where the buyer has the right to buy sterling at a strike price of 1·50 and the current spot price is 1·5275, then the intrinsic value is 2·75 cents. All this means is that a call option at 1·50 exercised today would provide an instant profit of 2·75 cents by selling the option proceeds into today's spot market. So, one way to think of intrinsic value is: 'the gain that would result if the option were exercised today'. It is useful when evaluating the relative attractiveness of various option premia to strip out the intrinsic value so that time value alone can be seen.

Time value is more complicated. It is a measure of the amount the exchange rate might be expected to move in the holder's favour during the balance of the time to run. It is therefore apparent that time value will depend not only on the time to expiry but also on the expected volatility of the exchange rate. The more volatile the exchange rate the greater the chance that a given level might be reached during the time left to run. It also follows from this reasoning that the greater the current loss at any time, i.e. the further the price will have to rise in order to profit from exercise of the option, the lower will the likelihood be of this happening so that the time premium will be correspondingly lower to reflect this.

A number of theoretical models have been used in the field of stock options which attempt to estimate time value depending on time to run and historical volatility. All these models produce a decay pattern for time value, whereby in the early days of an option time value falls slowly, but accelerates into an increasingly steep fall as the expiration date is neared. This general pattern also occurs for currency options, but as yet the modified stock options models do not seem to work very well for currencies. The theoretical models mostly assume that currency price movements against time follow a log normal distribution, which is the experience in stock markets, but currencies seem more wayward, in that they frequently display one way biases and also move discontinuously, such as upon devaluations. These factors create significant problems for the theoretical models presently in use, but no doubt modified versions will come into use which will allow for some of these problems and improve the accuracy of time value estimation.

Meanwhile market operators, never people to be overawed by theoreticians of any kind, continue to base their pricing on the ancient and well tested principle of simply seeing what they are able to sell the contract for at the time. Nevertheless, from the above we can establish certain general conclusions.

(i) The option premium may be thought of as the sum of the intrinsic value and the time value.

(ii) Intrinsic value is the profit that would arise if the option were exercised today.

(iii) Intrinsic value can never be negative, since at this level the option would not be exercised. (The buyer is under no obligation to exercise at a loss, and therefore presumably will not do so.)

(iv) Time value can never be negative, although it will fall continuously towards zero as expiration date approaches.

(v) At any given time there will be a choice of exercise prices and expiration dates in the market.

a: The further maturity dates will have higher premia than the near ones, because time value will be higher.

b: For call options, the higher the exercise price the lower the premium; intrinsic value will be lower.

c: For put options, the lower the exercise price the lower the premium; intrinsic value will be lower.

The above propositions provide an initial framework for option pricing, but we can take this a few steps further. We have seen how time value varies with time; now we take a look at how it varies with the exercise price. The first section of the table on p. 53 shows actual market prices for Deutsche mark options as at 22 August 1983. The second section takes the middle of the bid/ask premia and then splits them into the two components of intrinsic value and time value. It will be seen that the highest time value occurs at the nearest strike price to the current spot price of 37·93, i.e. 38. Why is this?

For ease of discussion let us consider the call option premia. It is readily apparent that if the price is now 37·93 then a strike price of 38 is more likely to be exceeded in the 117 days left to run than is a price of 40. In turn, a price of 40 has a greater chance of being exceeded than a price of 42. It is in fact generally true that the further out-of-the-money the option is the less the time value will be, owing to the reducing chance of seeing a profit in the time left to run.

Turning to the at-the-money option, this is really a one way bet; downward movement costs nothing, but upward movement is pure profit, hence time value is high. This is no longer the case for the in-the-money option because as time goes by some of the existing

December Deutsche Marks, as at 22 August 1983

Basic Quotes

Exercise Price	Calls	Puts
36	251/263	16/20
38	114/122	67/71
40	41/45	205/215
42	10/14	405/415

FX spot 37·93, outright to December 38·53 (117 days)

Intrinsic Value & Time Value

Exercise Price	Calls			Puts		
	Middle	Intrin	Time	Middle	Intrin	Time
36	257	193	64	18	—	18
38	118	—	118	69	7	62
40	43	—	43	210	207	3
42	12	—	12	410	407	3

Call/Put Spread & Forwards

E	C	P	C–P	F–E
Exercise Price	Call	Put		
36	257	18	239	253
38	118	69	49	53
40	43	210	(167)	(147)
42	12	410	(398)	(347)

Forward price, F = 38·53

unrealised profit could be lost – there is now a downside risk as well as an upside potential. Time value for in-the-money options will thus fall for options further into the money. Deeply in-the-money options may even have time values very close to zero. (The 42 put in the example shown is a case in point.)

5.5   Relationship to Forward FX Prices

The levels of option premia are further constrained by the possibilities of arbitrage with the forward foreign exchange market.

An outright forward foreign exchange contract would be represented on an options style profit chart by a diagonal straight line, rising from left to right. If the currency rises x% from the price dealt then proceeds will rise x% too; if the currency falls x% then proceeds will fall x%. So it behaves like buying a call on the upside, like selling a put on the downside. Indeed, buying a call and selling a put are together equivalent in effect to an outright forward purchase at the exercise price. This being the case, it would be expected that these two alternative routes would also be equivalent in cost.

The cost of the 'synthetic' forward contract is made up from the call premium paid, C, less the put premium received, P, and the exercise price agreed, E. The cost of an outright forward contract to the same date is F. So we would expect that:

$$F = E + (C - P), \text{ or}$$
$$(C - P) = (F - E)$$

This can be readily checked against actual market rates.

This has been done in the third section of the rates table shown earlier in this section, using prices for December Deutsche marks. It is seen that the correspondence between the two columns for $(C - P)$ and $(F - E)$ is fairly good, while naturally it is not perfect. Clearly, if the two columns were seriously out of line it would be possible to do arbitrage deals at a profit until the gap narrowed to that representing dealing costs. Several interesting consequences flow from this relationship:

    (i) The gap between call and put premia is fixed within a fairly narrow band by forward foreign exchange market prices.

    (ii) If the outright price is equal to the exercise price then put and call premia should be roughly equal.

    (iii) A lower limit for a call premium may be set as $(F - E)$ and for a put premium $(E - F)$; this arises by simple arithmetic since neither P nor C can be negative.

    (iv) For in the money options, since exercise can be made at any date and not just at the expiry date, the lower limit for call premia is more strictly defined as $(F - E)$ or $(S - E)$, whichever is the higher, where S is the spot price. For example, from the table, for 36 calls:

        $(S - E) = 3793 - 3600 = 193;$ $(F - E) = 253$

    $(F - E)$ is therefore the higher and forms the lower limit to the call premium, which is actually at 257. Similarly, for

OPTIONS/FORWARDS RELATIONSHIPS

buy call = buy fwd + buy put

buy put = sell fwd + buy call

sell call = sell fwd + sell put

sell put = buy fwd + sell call

buy fwd = buy call + sell put

sell fwd = buy put + sell call

puts the limit is $(E - F)$ or $(E - S)$ whichever is the higher. For 42 puts the figures are:

$$(E - F) = 347; \qquad (E - S) = 407$$

The 407 thus forms the lower limit; actual put premium is 410.

(v) A 'synthetic' for any forward contract can be created from two option contracts.

(vi) A 'synthetic' for any option contract can be created by a forward contract plus another option.

The chart 'Options/Forwards Relationships' on p. 55 shows the various possibilities for the creation of such 'synthetics'.

6 Using Currency Options

6.1 Advantages of Currency Options

Options have a number of advantages and disadvantages compared with forwards and futures markets; these comparative pros and cons between them define a 'niche' where options may be the best solution to the problem. It therefore seems logical that prior to discussing the various uses for options we should consider the pros and cons in order to identify those areas where options are likely to have a net advantage. The main advantages are:

a: Option buyers know at the outset what the 'worst case' will be; they pay their premium and no further expense is possible. Where it is necessary to limit the downside this is a powerful advantage.

b: Since there is no obligation to exercise an option, options are ideal for hedging contingent cash flows which may or may not materialise, such as in tenders.

c: Options provide a very flexible means of currency cover, offering a range of strike prices; forward and futures markets only deal at the forward price existing now.

d: Options provide another possibility in the range of tools available to treasurers and traders. They can be used alone to achieve types of cover not otherwise possible and they can be used in conjunction with the forward and futures markets to achieve more complex aims.

e: Options may be used as a 'ratchet', to lock up profit to date on a currency position while retaining any remaining upside potential.

f: Futures require margin and daily mark to market to cover credit risk, forwards require a credit line from a bank, an option buyer needs neither.

The main disadvantages are:

a: Compared to ordinary forward cover, options are expensive, especially when commissions are taken into account.

b: As yet, only a limited range of currencies is available.

c: Expiration dates and strike prices are standardised in the traded markets, and these may not correspond to those that would be ideal for a particular situation. (Although bank options can be tailormade, see **6.5** on p. 68.)

6.2 Hedging for a Tender

The classic 'ideal' use for currency options is the tender situation. Here a firm makes an offer to supply at a fixed currency price and holds this offer open for a period of time. During this time the firm is at risk to currency movements, but cannot economically take out forward cover – to do so could give rise to a loss if the order were lost. Effectively the tenderer gives his potential customer a currency option for as long as the offer remains open; the only way he can achieve precise cover is by the use of another, offsetting option.

It will be recognised that the tender situation does not only occur in major multi-million construction projects, it is also there whenever a supplier makes an offer to a prospective customer in ordinary trading, and it lasts until the offer is accepted or rejected. All currency price lists come into this category. Further, tender situations are not only present in trading but arise in many capital investment transactions too, from buying a new machine right up to bidding to acquire a foreign company. The common theme is that a currency risk is incurred which is contingent in nature; cover is required which is similarly contingent in nature – there if required but not otherwise.

Hedging Example for a Tender
Consider a manufacturer whose costs are in US dollars, who is

required to tender for a possible export order in Swiss francs. It is May, and his quotation will be outstanding until December before he will know whether or not he has been successful in obtaining the order. To achieve his target profit he has to realise a dollar sum of $120,000. What should he do about the currency risk? There are at least four possible approaches which we now take in turn.

Case 1. Normal Forward Cover
Sell Swiss francs and buy dollars for delivery end of December. Spot exchange rate is CHF 1 = $0·4941.
Outright exchange rate is CHF 1 = $0·5085.
Required selling price = CHF 120,000/0·5085 = CHF 235,988.
(This same price will be used for the other approaches too, for ease of comparison.)

This will achieve a neutral result if the contract is won, but an unknown result if the contract is lost. If this happens and the Swiss franc falls 10%, the exporter will gain $12,000; if it rises 10% he will lose $12,000. Furthermore, the downside risk is unlimited; it simply depends on how far the Swiss franc moves.

Case 2. Masterly Inactivity
Price as above and then do nothing. If the contract is lost the risk disappears; if the contract is won then we are in the same risk situation as above, but reversed. This makes more sense than Case 1 if the odds of getting the contract are rated below evens. But the downside risk is still unlimited.

Case 3. Use Put Options
Here options are brought to put (sell) Swiss francs next December. Current rates are:

Currency Option Premia, Dec Swiss Francs, 13 May.

Strike	Call Premia	Put Premia
46	485	19
48	336	55
50	180	197

Spot: 49·41, Forward: 50·85

From this we can see that we are able to obtain 4 put contracts of CHF 62,500 each at a strike price of 48 for a premium of 55 points/contract.

Premium/contract = 55 × $6·25 = $343·75
Plus brokerage of, say $50·00
Total premium on 4 contracts = ($343·75 + $50) × 4 = $1575
It should be noted here that:

    a: The $1575 is spent at the outset and is a straight expense. There is no initial expense in forward contracts as no money passes until maturity. The interest cost of option premia from expenditure until maturity is ignored in this example.

    b: We have no cover for the initial range of movement from the current outright price of 50·85 down to the option price of 48.

    c: Ideally cover should be taken for $235,988, but since we can only deal in whole contracts we have an option for the slightly greater amount of $250,000.

We can now look at the four possible outcomes:
order won, Swiss franc rises
order won, Swiss franc falls
order lost, Swiss franc rises
order lost, Swiss franc falls

Case 3 outcomes

(A) Put Option, Economics if Order Won

    (i) If Swiss franc rises 10% to 0·5435

Sell CHF 235,988 at 0·5435	$128,259
Less required return	($120,000)
Deduct cost of option	($1,575)
Net Gain	$6,684

    (ii) If Swiss franc falls 10% to 0·4492

Sell CHF 235,988 at 0·4492	$106,006
Less required return	($120,000)
Gain on option (0·48 − 0·4492)	$7,700
Deduct cost of option	($1,575)
Net Loss	$7,869

(B) Put Option, Economics if Order Lost

    (i) If Swiss franc rises 10% to 0·5435

Cost of option	($1,575)

(ii) If Swiss franc falls 10% to 0·4492

Gain on option, as above	$7,700
Deduct cost of option	($1,575)
Net Gain	$6,125

Case 4. Forward Sale and Call Option
Here the approach is to sell the CHF 235,988 forward as in Case 1, but also to take out a call option to offset it to be used if required. At the quoted rates it is possible to obtain December call options at a strike price of 50 at a premium of 180 points.

Premium/contract = $ 6·25 × 180 = $1125
Plus brokerage, say $ 50
Cost of 4 contracts = (1125 + 50) × 4 = $4700

Case 4 outcomes
(A) Call Option, Economics if Order Won

(i) If Swiss franc rises 10% to 0·5435

Forward contract proceeds	$120,000
Less required return	($120,000)
Gain on option (·5435 − ·50)	$10,875
Deduct cost of option	($4,700)
Net Gain	$6,175

(ii) If Swiss franc falls 10% to 0·4492

Cost of option	($4,700)

(B) Call Option, Economics if Order Lost

(i) If Swiss franc rises 10% to 0·5435

Forward contract proceeds	$120,000
Buy CHF 235,988 at 0·5435	($128,259)
Gain on call option as A(i)	$10,875
Deduct cost of option	($4,700)
Net Loss	$2,084

(ii) If Swiss franc falls 10% to 0·4492

Forward contract proceeds	$120,000
Buy CHF 235,988 at 0·4492	($106,006)
Deduct option cost	($4,700)
Net Gain	$9,294

Now we have come this far, it is time to examine what we have established to date.

	1 Forward Cover	2 Do Nothing	3 Put Option	4 Call +Cover
Summary of Results, $				
(A) Contract Won				
(i) CHF 10% up	—	12,000	6,684	6,175
(ii) CHF 10% down	—	(12,000)	(7,869)	(4,700)
(B) Contract Lost				
(i) CHF 10% up	(12,000)	—	(1,575)	(2,084)
(ii) CHF 10% down	12,000	—	6,125	9,294
Average outcome	nil	nil	841	2,171
Worst case	no limit	no limit	(7,869)	(4,700)

Some important points are:

a: Forward cover is no better than total inaction, even supposing the odds of getting the contract are evens. Usually the odds are somewhat poorer than this (few firms expect to succeed on a majority of tenders), and if so, total inaction will actually be cheaper than forward cover. But neither method can really be considered as at all satisfactory – in both cases there is a possibility of unlimited loss depending on how far the Swiss franc happens to move during the tender period.

b: Both of the option based methods are appreciably better, both as measured by the average return on the four possible outcomes and, more importantly, as measured by the worst possible outcome.

c: Note that if currency swings were doubled to 20%, gains on the option based methods would be doubled, but losses would stay exactly the same as shown.

d: There is no absolute rule that suggests that Case 4 will always be more attractive than Case 3. Sometimes it is not. But method 4 retains the ability to cover the exact amount to the exact date, which is an important operational advantage over method 3.

e: A put option could be substituted for the forward contract in method 4, but this would usually be a little more expensive and would forgo the exact amount, exact date advantage mentioned above.

Possible Refinements

It is of course a simple matter in theory to eliminate all possibility of a loss on a winning tender by increasing the selling price to include the cost of the option. This, however desirable, may or may not be commercially feasible if competitors do not price this way too. (Although it may be reasonably assumed that competitors may price on the forward rate so that the 'option cost' is only the net of the option premium and the forward premium, rather than the entire option premium.) Even so, this method would not protect the tenderer against the smaller loss of the type B(i) (see p. 61) arising on a losing tender.

Again, in theory, this loss could be taken out by 'gearing up the option', i.e. taking out six option contracts rather than four so as to put Case B(i) back into profit. So it will, but the average return on all four outcomes will fall and it may not be thought worthwhile.

A more useful line of development suggests itself where the tenderer has a view as to the relative likelihood of the four outcomes. If they are not all judged equally likely, as has been the implicit assumption in the foregoing analysis, then it is possible to consider tailoring the hedge to maximise the expected outcome on a statistical basis, allowing different weights to the four possible outcomes and maximising their weighted sum.

6.3   Options for Trade Cover

Options may be used in the same way as forward contracts to hedge trade payables and receivables in currency. Yet there is an important difference in the type of cover obtained. Importers are typically urged to use forward cover so as to fix the cost of their imports in sterling terms. The bankers advising them to do so no doubt believe they are giving good conservative advice in this respect and may be puzzled why the importer does not always seem to keen to cover. It is not because they are stupid.

The importer may not in fact be concerned to fix his cost *per se*, he may actually wish to be sure that his costs are no worse than his competition. Forward cover may or may not achieve this. If he covers and (either through careful assessment of the risks, good luck or sheer neglect) his competitor does not, his competitor may deal at a better rate than he does and sell the goods cheaper than he can. If so, the importer will have to cut his prices to remain competitive. Forward cover thus protects the financial risk only; not the commercial risk.

Option cover protects against the actual commercial risk, protecting the downside while retaining the benefits of any upside movement in the rate.

Consider the position of a UK importer purchasing paper from the USA at a price of $520,000. It is August and payment is due in December. The importer cannot afford to take the risk of having no cover, yet feels the dollar may weaken by year end. He decides that he could accept a limited downside of a cent or so in the exchange rate and elects to cover using put options in sterling.

Prices for December puts are:

Strike Price, c	Premium, pts
145	130
150	170
155	510

Spot and outright to December are both 1·5160.

His sterling cost if he were to cover in the forward market would be $520,000/1·5160 = 343,007·91 no matter what the exchange rate was in December. This would eliminate all downside risk, but would also eliminate any upside potential. Being prepared to accept a worst case of 1·50 (and possibly planning to set his UK selling prices based on a rate of 1·50 in any case), he takes out 27 sterling December puts at a strike price of 150, and a premium of 170 points. The arithmetic is:

No. of contracts = $520,000/1·5160 × 1/12,500
= 27·44, say 27

Premium = 170 × 12,500 × 1/10,000 × 27 = $5,737·50, or at 1·5160, GBP 3, 784·63.

Ignoring commission costs and the slight mismatch in the amount, the possible outcomes now are:

  a: As expected, the dollar weakens to, say, 1·65. The defensive option expires worthless. He buys the $520,000 in the spot market at 1·65.

cost of dollars in cash market	GBP 315,151·51
option premium paid	GBP 3,784·63
total cost	GBP 318,936·14

This is a gain of GBP 24,071·77 versus the forward cover route.

b: His view was wrong and the dollar strengthens to, say, 1·42. The option is exercised at 1·50 to provide the 'worst case' cost as below:

proceeds from exercise of option	GBP 346,666·67
option premium paid	GBP 3,784·63
total cost	GBP 350,451·30

This a loss of GBP 7,443·39 versus the forward cover route.

Many treasurers will find this combination of containable and often affordable downside plus retention of all of the upside potential to be a very attractive proposition.

There are of course two principal disadvantages:

a: He starts off with a worse effective exchange rate for cover than with forwards; here $1·50 - 0·0170 = 1·4830$ as against $1·5160$ for forwards. So that sterling will have to rise by 3·3 cents before he will be better off than forward cover.

b: He has to pay the option premium up front, which is a minor cash flow disadvantage.

But there is a further argument in favour of the option route which perhaps owes more to human frailty than cool business logic, but is no less important for that. In the situation above, had it been hedged with forward contracts then the business would have no risk at all. If the dollar rose the cost rose but this was offset by the gain on the forward contract; if the dollar fell the cost fell but this was offset by the loss on the forward contract. All in all, then, a successful hedge. Yet in the latter case it is only human to ask the treasurer to account for 'his' loss on 'his' forward contracts. The firm would have been better off without them would it not? What is his advice for next time? And so on.

Somehow the 'insurance' premium of an option is much easier to sell internally as a sensible defence against catastrophe, especially since the upside remains intact. If the premium comes to be regarded as part of the cost of doing business, then the treasurer no longer has any downside at all; sometimes he will seem to break even, other times notch up a success. Options are not necessarily the cheapest way to cover trade flows, but are very tempting nonetheless.

6.4   Which Option to Buy

When a treasurer has decided to cover a particular currency exposure by means of, say, a call option, he is still faced with the problem of which option to buy. Like forward and futures markets there is a range of different maturities, but for options there is also a range of different strike prices and their associated premia.

Choosing the Date

The examples so far have all assumed that there was an option contract maturing on the same date as the cash item to be covered and that this option would be used to achieve cover.

Whereas the above method is the simplest and indeed the most usual one, it is possible to choose options of much later maturity than the cash item. Taking options which are longer than the underlying cash maturity date involves a tradeoff between two opposing factors.

We have seen in **5.4** on p. 50 that, if spot prices remain steady, then time value over the life of an option falls slowly at first and then falls increasingly steeply towards zero at the expiration date. Thus, although time values will be higher for longer dated contracts, it may be that the fall in time value during the life of the hedge will be less than for the nearer dated contract. This is because on the date the hedge is closed the option will still have many months to run and will not yet be into the steeper part of the time value decay curve.

The risks with this approach concern the difficulty of estimating this residual time value. Strictly, an option hedge is only perfect when the dates of the cash position and the option coincide, so that time value is zero on maturity. Since time value will be zero, no 'estimate' of its residual value is necessary, nor can there be any range of error on that estimate. When an option is closed out near to its expiration date, time value is likely to be very small whatever the spot price is and so the effect on the hedge efficiency is negligible, but when far dated options are used residual time value may be large or small depending on the spot price when closed out. (As discussed in **5.4**, time value varies depending on where the spot price is relative to the exercise price.) The effect of this variability of time value is that if the option moves further into the money, time value will fall and so offset part of the improvement in intrinsic value. The total value of the option (being time value + intrinsic value) will therefore move somewhat less than $1 for a $1 change in the spot price. Generally then, where there is a date mismatch between the option and the underlying cash with the option the longer dated, more than the nominal quantity of options is required to produce a 'neutral' hedge. The resultant problem is twofold; it is very difficult to estimate accurately the amount by which the hedge should be factored up to achieve a neutral hedge (although formulae exist to do this approximately), and, secondly, since more options are required, the aggregate premium cost goes up.

Choosing the Strike Price

It must be said at the outset that there is no mechanical method for establishing the 'best buy' between the strike prices available at any given time. The most appropriate strike price for a given user, however, may be more reliably determined. The key questions are:

(i) What is the option buyer's tolerance of risk?

(ii) What does he expect currency movements to be during the life of the option?

It is simplest to illustrate the issues involved using actual premia. Those for sterling December calls on 19 August 1983 were:

(a) strike price, c	(b) premium, pts	(c) = (a) + (b) breakeven price
145	560	1·5060
150	320	1·5320
155	140	1·5640
160	60	1·6060
	spot:	1·4970

The breakeven price is simply the sum of the strike price and the premium; commissions are ignored.

A risk averse hedger will normally take the at-the-money option, here the 150 strike price, since this will most exactly hedge his cash risk. But if he is prepared to take some of the risk himself he will go for an out-of-the-money option, say 155 in order to save on premium costs. Even further, the less concerned hedger, who can accept sizeable fluctuations in the rate, but merely requires protection against really major adverse swings – 'disaster insurance' – will go for a far out-of-the-money option contract such as the 160, which will be very cheap in premium terms.

Position takers or speculators will view it rather differently, something after the fashion of choosing which horse to back in the Derby. Out-of-the-money contracts are very cheap, but give very low prospects of a gain – this is the 20–1 outsider in the race. In-the-money options have high premia *vis-à-vis* any possible gain, but the chances of the gain occurring are proportionately higher – the equivalent of the odds-on favourite. The choice here boils down to the degree of risk the speculator is prepared to take and his expectation of the size of rate movements.

6.5   Options from Banks

Currency options are increasingly becoming available from banks. Bank options may be made more flexible than those traded on exchanges as they can be tailormade to particular strike prices, expiration dates and amounts to suit the customer, and need not be constricted by any externally defined contract specification.

Banks may take the risk on their own books, or, more usually, 'marry' it against offsetting contracts with other customers; lay it off in part or in whole with other banks, or with options exchanges such as Philadelphia. The bank's ability to lay off the deal and so limit its own exposure is obviously limited by the extent to which the options it writes correspond to exchange traded option specifications although as interbank trading develops this may not remain the case. Tailor-made deals are thus likely to be more expensive the more non-standard they are, as the bank's risk is higher; the irreducible residual risk inevitably reflects itself in the premium.

Even if the treasurer is content to cover risk only on an approximate basis by dealing for exact multiples of standard Philadelphia contracts, it may still be more advantageous to deal with a bank than with an options exchange. For most companies, with only sporadic requirements to use options, it will not be worthwhile to set up accounts with Philadelphia brokers and to go through the necessary paperwork and Board Resolutions to do so; commission rates depend heavily on volume and an active bank will always be able to trade on the market more cheaply than its customers. The major advantage of bank options is thus convenience, whether dealing for standard or tailormade options; the treasurer simply calls his bank, pays up the premium and receives a normal advice of the deal done in the same way as for any other foreign exchange transaction.

A theoretical disadvantage of using tailormade options is that, being non-standard, they can in effect only be sold back to the institution where they were bought; there is a consequent concern that since the treasurer effectively has nowhere else to go, he may get a poor price when he does elect to sell back. This is less of a problem in the real commercial world, for both parties know that if the customer is not satisfied with the service he receives he can deal elsewhere next time round and accordingly any bank wishing to develop a successful options business will ensure that its customers receive good sell-back prices for their options. (Nor should it be supposed that the 'trapped customer' worry only applies to bank options – an exchange traded option bought through a particular broker can only be sold back via that same broker.)

The bank options described above offer all the characteristics of exchange traded options as regards pricing and saleability together with the additional flexibilities created by the user's ability to choose strike prices, amounts and maturities to exactly suit his purposes.

There also exists a more limited type of option offered by certain banks known as an 'exercise only' option. Such options have a more restricted use for corporate treasurers as they cannot be sold back, although initial premia are usually lower than for a full option. In particular, since an 'exercise only' option when exercised only yields intrinsic value and no time value at all, it may be unattractive where:

(i) there is a possibility that the user may wish to exercise the option prior to maturity, for instance, when covering contingent cash flows which may or may not arise, since all residual time value will be 'thrown away';

(ii) or the buyer wishes to use an 'out of the money' option (as many corporate users will). Here, unless the exchange rate moves sufficiently far to become 'in the money' the option will have no value on exercise; an equivalent 'saleable option' would increase in value as the exchange rate moved favourably to any extent, whether or not it moved far enough to reach the strike price, and this value increase would be realisable when sold back.

6.6 Writing Options

Writing options should not be lightly undertaken; it can involve a potentially unlimited risk. Nevertheless, for every buyer of an option there has to be an option writer. There are three principal types of option writing:

(i) Option writing as a professional business.

(ii) 'Covered' writing against positions.

(iii) Writing as part of a 'combination deal'.

The first category is a business akin to the insurance business, receiving a steady premium income which is judged to be in excess of predicted claims experience. It is apparent that this requires both capital to cope with periods of high claims and a large, balanced book spread over calls and puts in a variety of currencies to provide an element of averaging. It is a business for professionals. The third category will be discussed in **6.7** and **6.8**, leaving us to discuss covered writing in this section.

Covered writing involves writing, say, call options in Swiss francs against an existing holding of Swiss francs. Here the writer is covered in the sense that, if the Swiss franc rises he has no loss since he only undertakes to sell currency he already possesses. (He has of course an opportunity cost since, had he not written the option, he would have benefited from the rise in the Swiss franc.)

Writing covered call options is used by investors to enhance the return on currency which they would hold in any case, 'natural holders of the currency'. Consider such an investor, perhaps a Swiss insurance company, who would normally have substantial funds in Swiss francs, currently earning a return of say 4·5% per annum. Using the rates from **6.2**, spot price is 49·41 cents/CHF and calls at 50 can be written for a premium of 180 points, or $1125 per contract. Over the 7-month period of the option, at the current dollar value of the contract $(62,500 \times ·4941) = \$30,881·25$, this is worth an additional return of:

$$1125/30,881·25 \times 12/7 \times 100 = 6·245\% \text{ per annum}$$

This gives a total return of 10·745%. If the Swiss franc remains at current levels or falls then the above return will be achieved. If the Swiss franc rises and the option is exercised, then the writer delivers the Swiss francs at the strike price of 50. Since he retains the premium his effective selling price is 51·80, which still compares favourably with the 49·41 prevailing when he wrote the option.

Covered writers must bear in mind that their currency must be truly liquid, since the option buyer has the right to exercise his option and demand delivery of the currency at any time. (He may not of course find it attractive to do this until near the expiration date, since he will fare better by selling the option to collect the time value; the point is that he has the right to demand exercise if he so wishes.)

A further, perhaps rather obvious point, but one that can be overlooked, is that options can only be written against funds which are essentially uncommitted for any other purpose. For instance, if the reason the Swiss francs were held was to meet some future payment in Swiss francs then the funds cannot also be available to meet an option buyer's call.

6.7   Using Combinations

Having examined the outline economics of simple call and put options, we now look at the way these options can be used together in combinations. Professional option traders can use a bewildering array of sophisticated option strategies but here we will consider only the two most commonly used combinations, 'spreads' and 'straddles'.

Call Spreads
A call spread is the combination of a buy and a write of call options, at different strike prices. The call spread may be regarded as essentially writing a call option, and then spending part of the· premium received on buying a cheaper call to limit the downside risk. Call spreads make money if the currency weakens, and may thus also be termed 'bear spreads'. As usual, it is much easier to understand the concepts involved by means of a diagram: a profit chart for a call spread is shown on p. 72. It is based on the premia already used in **6.2**:

December Swiss franc options, 13 May 1983. Spot 49·41

Strike	Call Premia	Put Premia
46	485	19
48	336	55
50	180	197

PROFIT CHART FOR CALL SPREAD
December, Swiss Francs

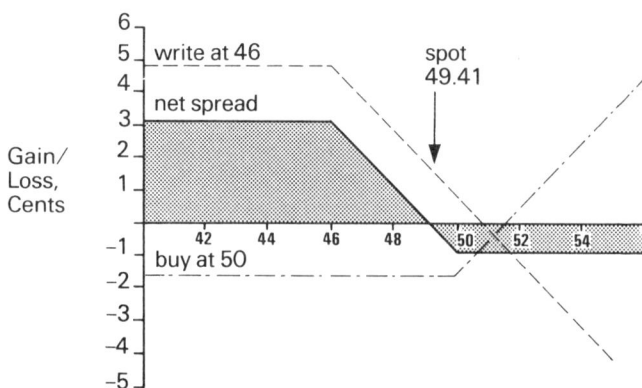

The investor writes a 46 call and receives 485 points in premium, he then pays out 180 points to buy a 50 call, a net income of 305 points. It will be seen from the chart that, if the Swiss franc is weaker than 46, neither option will be exercised and the investor will have secured the 305 points as net profit. If the investor's bearish view was wrong and the Swiss franc moves to 50 or more, he cannot lose more than 95 points, calculated as:

Net premium, 305 − difference in strike prices, 400 = − 95

For prices between 46 and 50, his profit varies between the + 305 and − 95 points in a pro rata manner as shown in the profit chart.

Put Spreads
Put spreads operate in an identical manner, writing a put and spending part of the premium on buying a cheaper put. Put spreads are bullish. Using the same table of premia, it would be possible to write a 50 put at 197 and buy a 46 put at 19. The maximum gain here is 178 points and the maximum loss is 178 − 400 = 222 points − apparently a rather less attractive prospect than the call spread which no doubt reflected a prevailing market view that the Swiss franc was more likely to go up than down.

Straddles

Straddles have no real equivalent in other markets; they are not a bet on whether a currency will go up or down, but rather a bet on how far the currency will move from its present rate. Straddles are a means to take a view about volatility. A straddle buyer buys both a put and a call, a straddle writer writes both a put and a call.

PROFIT CHART FOR BUYING A STRADDLE
December, Swiss Francs

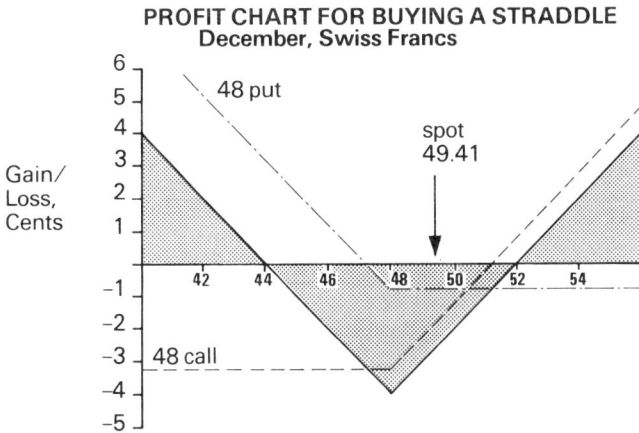

Buying a Straddle

Expects high volatility; if rates stay at or close to present levels a loss will result. The profit chart shows a straddle using the 48 strike price premia from the same table as above. Profits result if the spot price is outside the range 44·09 to 51·91, losses result within this range. The calculations are:

48 call premium	336
48 put premium	55
Move from 48 to break even	391

So breakeven at 48 + 3·91 cents, or 48 − 3·91 cents.

Writing a Straddle

Buying a straddle has limited downside and theoretically unlimited upside. Writing a straddle has unlimited downside in both directions. Writing straddles is therefore dangerous: both options may be exercised against the writer during the period of the deal if the currency moves up then down.

A 'strangle' is market jargon for a straddle with unequal exercise prices.

6.8 Conversions and Reversals

Section **5.5** (p. 53) explained the correspondence between forward foreign exchange rates and option prices; conversions and reversals are transactions based on this equivalence which produce 'synthetic' forward exchange contracts.

A synthetic forward bought contract is created by buying a call and selling a put. If this works out cheaper than the forward or futures market, then the synthetic bought contract, or 'synthetic long' can be matched at a profit by an offsetting sale in the forward or futures market. This combination deal is a conversion.

The equivalent arbitrage, creating a synthetic short by buying a put and selling a call, and then buying the offsetting forward or future, is a reversal.

For obvious reasons these types of transactions tend to be confined to professional market operators, but there is one byproduct of the process which is of more general use to treasurers. Because conversion and reversal activity maintains price equivalence between the options, forwards, and futures markets it is possible to transform existing call options into puts or *vice versa*, using the forward or future markets. The relationships are:

call option + forward sale = put option
put option + forward purchase = call option

7 Introduction to Financial Futures

Note

The next three chapters concern financial futures. This chapter is about the mechanics of the market itself; chapters 8 and 9 are about ways in which treasurers may use the market either for trading or as an exposure management tool. Although much of the material will be of relevance to financial futures markets generally, where specific detail is involved we will discuss the market with reference to the London International Financial Futures Exchange (LIFFE).

7.1 Purpose of the Market

The purpose of the financial futures markets is to enable companies and individuals to fix in advance interest and exchange rates whose variability might otherwise adversely impact upon them. The prime purpose, then, is to hedge business against adverse movements in interest or exchange rates. The exchange itself provides a place where the buying and selling may be conducted and so provides a means to set prices for these transactions. The commodity being bought and sold in such a market is a 'Financial Future'. Before going any further, this concept must be defined.

Definition

'A financial future is a standard contract between buyer and seller, in which the buyer has a binding obligation to buy

> a fixed amount (the contract size)
> at a fixed price (the futures price)
> on a fixed date (the delivery date)
> of some underlying security.'

The 'underlying security' for the financial future contract may be anything from a quantity of foreign currency, to a bond, or a three month time deposit. For each class of underlying security traded or 'contract' there is a detailed contract specification laid down by the exchange which defines precisely what is contracted to be bought or sold.

Futures exchanges have fixed delivery dates. In the case of LIFFE these are, for most contracts, the second Wednesday of each of the months of March, June, September and December. No other delivery dates may be dealt for. In this way the market turnover is concentrated on only four dates, and the chances of finding a counterparty for a given deal in the market are greatly increased. For the same reason of ease of matching buyers and sellers, each type of contract is defined in amount (e.g. for the Eurodollar deposit contract the contract size is one million dollars). Trading may only be conducted in round numbers of contracts; part contracts cannot be traded. Indeed, a trader will not say 'I bought $2m of eurodollar contracts'; he will say 'I bought two contracts in the eurodollar'.

7.2 Market Structure

The structure of a futures exchange is surprisingly complex, as many different types of organisations are involved with different rôles to play in the conduct of the business of the market.

Firstly there is the Exchange itself, LIFFE, which provides the physical facilities for trading and the organisational infrastructure to enable futures contracts to be struck. The Exchange is responsible for:

a: providing premises for trading

b: providing communications and other ancillary equipment required by traders

c: selection of the member firms and ensuring that members are suitably screened on application as to their financial standing and adequacy of capital resources

d: establishing rules of conduct and market practice

e: defining contract terms

f: establishing procedures and systems for traders

g: monitoring trading activity

The Exchange was originally financed by the sale of memberships to the original subscribers in 1982 and on a current basis receives an income from the members by way of

(i) a fee on each contract traded on the exchange, and

(ii) an annual fee in respect of each trader and other employee of a member authorised by the exchange to operate on the floor of the exchange, and

(iii) rental of certain facilities within the exchange, such as trading booths.

The Exchange itself does not in any way handle the payments associated with the contracts struck; this rôle is carried out separately by the International Commodities Clearing House, ICCH, an organisation owned by the London clearing banks. Broadly speaking, the clearing house is responsible for everything that happens after the original deal has been struck on the exchange. In turn, this rôle may be roughly summarised as matching, margin, and maturities. These aspects are now considered in turn.

When a deal is struck on the exchange copies of the deal tickets of buyer and seller are handed to the exchange clerk for immediate entry into the clearing house computer. The first task is to check that the details as given by the two counterparties do in fact match one another. At this point let us suppose that Member A has sold one Gilt contract to Member B for delivery in June. The ICCH computer checks that both parties to the deal have recorded the same price, that they both agree that the contract traded was the Gilt contract, in quantity one contract, for delivery June, with one seller, A, and one buyer, B. So far so good. But now something quite fundamental to the operation of the market occurs.

ICCH now interposes itself between buyer and seller. From this point on Member A is deemed to have sold to ICCH, and Member B is deemed to have bought from ICCH. What has this achieved? Firstly, Member A no longer has to concern himself with the credit risk on Member B; his counterparty is (and for all trades on the market always will be) ICCH. But ICCH, having at all times bought precisely what it has sold has no market risk at any time. So Member A, and Member B, will find that their credit risk is solely with ICCH, which they should be perfectly relaxed about as a risk since they are aware that ICCH has no net position, and that in any case ICCH is a well capitalised organisation owned by the clearing banks. But ICCH is left with a genuine credit risk on all the members it has dealt with, and this remaining risk is removed by the system of 'margin'.

Margin is discussed in more detail in **7.5** on p. 82 but for the moment it will be simply stated that a member is required to put up a cash deposit or 'margin' with the clearing house in respect of every contract he has outstanding at any time. The margin is made up of two components, initial margin which is on a simple fixed scale per contract laid down by the clearing house, and variation margin which is equal to the unrealised gain or loss on contracts outstanding when valued at today's prices. ICCH is responsible for calculating margin due to or from members and ensuring that payment is made. In this way all members pay in their unrealised loss to ICCH daily with the result that the credit exposure of the clearing house towards each individual member is nil.

ICCH is also responsible for laying down procedures to be followed in the event of futures contracts running to maturity and requiring actual delivery and in calculating amounts due in the event of cash settlements.

Only members of the exchange are permitted to transact business on the floor of the exchange. Business must be transacted between them by open outcry in a designated area of the floor known as a pit. There is a different pit for every contract being traded on the exchange in order to segregate out the activity between the different contracts. A trade between two members is only valid if conducted by open outcry within the confines of the relevant trading pit.

Member firms in turn may or may not also be members of the clearing house, but members who are not must make arrangements to clear their business through a member who is – a 'clearing member'. Some member firms may only deal for other members with no external customers, such firms are known as 'floor brokers'. Most members, particularly the larger, clearing members, are in business to transact the business of their customers on the exchange, and indeed any firm wishing to deal on the exchange is obliged to do so through a member firm.

A member firm trading on the floor of the exchange will typically have a booth on the perimeter of the trading floor for use as a local operating base. A booth contains telephone lines back to head office and external telephone lines as well as various VDU screens providing news services and data as to current prices on the exchange. The booth will be staffed by the member's 'booth man', whose job it is to receive incoming phone calls from clients or from head office concerning trades requiring execution. Such an order is conveyed to the member's trader in the relevant pit by a junior or 'runner' who gives the order by hand to the pit trader. The trader deals and gives the details of the deal done to the runner for return to the booth.

These three rôles of booth man, runner, and pit trader, will make up most of those present on the trading floor at any time, but, in addition to these, there are also exchange staff supervising the trading, ironing out problems and generally helping to ensure an orderly market.

7.3 LIFFE Contracts

Seven contracts were traded on LIFFE during its first year of operation. They are made up as follows:

- four contracts for currency exchange rates, available for sterling, deutschemark, Swiss franc, and Japanese yen, all versus the US$.
- two 3 month interest rate contracts, for domestic sterling and for eurodollars
- a 20 year Gilt contract

A summary of these contracts, issued by LIFFE and reproduced here with their permission, is shown on page 80. The outline of these contracts has remained substantially unchanged since their original introduction, but minor details, such as levels of margin, have varied from time to time.

New contracts are constantly under discussion and it is possible that at least three new contracts may be introduced at a later date:

- a stock index contract based on the FTSE 100 index.
- a 5 year eurobond contract with a contract size of $100,000.
- a 3 month euro deutschemark deposit contract with a contract size of possibly DM 1 million.

7.4 LIFFE Arithmetic

Prices are quoted on different conventions on LIFFE than in the cash markets, and although this is useful for market participants, undoubtedly the fact that prices are thus rendered less recognisable to

LIFFE

THE LONDON INTERNATIONAL
FINANCIAL FUTURES EXCHANGE

SUMMARY OF CONTRACTS

CONTRACT	THREE MONTH EURODOLLAR INTEREST RATE	THREE MONTH STERLING INTEREST RATE	TWENTY YEAR GILT INTEREST RATE	CURRENCIES £ DM SW.FR. YEN
UNIT OF TRADING	U.S.$1,000,000	£250,000	A notional stock - 20 years maturity with coupon of 12% £50,000 nominal value	25,000 125,000 125,000 12,500,000
CONTRACT STANDARD	(1) A three-month Eurodollar deposit facility arranged by the seller at one of a list of banks in London designated by the Exchange as deliverable names or (2) A cash settlement, at the buyer's option, based on the delivery settlement price ascertained and quoted by the Exchange.	(1) A three-month Sterling deposit facility arranged by the seller at one of a list of banks in London designated by the Exchange as deliverable names or (2) A cash settlement, at the buyer's option, based on the delivery settlement price ascertained and quoted by the Exchange.	(1) Delivery may be made of any gilt with 15-25 years to maturity. Stocks with an optional redemption date will be considered to have an outstanding term to the first redemption date. (2) Stocks must be delivered in multiples of £50,000 nominal. (3) No variable rate, index-linked, convertible or partly-paid gilts may be delivered. (4) Stocks are not deliverable within the period of three weeks and one day before the xd date. (5) Interest must be payable half-yearly.	Currencies will be deliverable in the principal financial centres in the country of issue.
DELIVERY MONTHS	SAME FOR ALL CONTRACTS i.e. March, June, September and December.			
DELIVERY DAY	Second Wednesday of delivery month. (If this is not a business day in London and New York then delivery is to be effected on the next business day common to both London and New York.)	Second Wednesday of delivery month. (If the second Wednesday is not a London business day, then the next business day will become delivery day.)	Any business day in delivery calendar month.	Second Wednesday of delivery month. (If this is not a business day in London and in the designated delivery centres then delivery is to be effected on the next business day common to London and the relevant delivery centre.)
WHEN SPOT	First day of the delivery month.	First day of the delivery month.	Seven business days before the start of the delivery month.	First day of the delivery month.
LAST TRADING DAY	Two business days common to both London and New York prior to delivery. (On this day trading ceases at 11.00 a.m. and will be for cash settlement only.)	The business day prior to delivery. (On this day trading ceases at 11.00 a.m. and will be for cash settlement only.)	Two business days prior to the end of the delivery month. (Trading ceases at 11.00 a.m. on this day.)	The second business day common to both London and the relevant delivery centre prior to delivery. Trading in the contracts ceases on this day at: 10.31a.m. 10.32a.m. 10.33a.m. 10.30a.m.
QUOTATION	100.00 minus the annual rate of interest in basis points i.e. 1 basis point is equivalent to 0.01%.	100.00 minus the annual rate of interest in basis points i.e. 1 basis point is equivalent to 0.01%.	Price per £100 nominal.	Price in U.S.$ per unit of currency.
MINIMUM PRICE MOVEMENT (i.e. TICK SIZE & VALUE)	One basis point, i.e. 0.01% (U.S.$25).	One basis point, i.e. 0.01% (£6.25).	£1/32 per £100 nominal (£15.625).	0.01 0.01 0.01 0.01 Cents Cents Cents Cents per per per per £1 1 DM 1 SW.FR. 100 YEN Equal to $2.50 $12.50 $12.50 $12.50
PRICE LIMIT*	100 basis points (U.S.$2,500).	100 basis points (£625.00).	£2 per £100 nominal (£1,000).	5 1 1 1 Cents Cent Cent Cent (All equal to $1,250)
INITIAL MARGIN**	U.S.$1,000 which is the equivalent of a 0.4% movement in interest rates. Straddle $750.	£500 which is the equivalent of a 0.8% movement in interest rates. Straddle £250.	£1,500 which is 3% of contract nominal value. Straddle £250.	$1,000 – Same for all contracts Straddle $375.
EXCHANGE DELIVERY SETTLEMENT PRICE	Based on an average, less 0.25% of the offer rates to prime banking names stated by a random sample of designated banks taken between 9.30 a.m. and 11.00 a.m. on the last trading day. The settlement price will be 100.00 minus the rate thus obtained. Differences between the settlement rate and the actual rate on the deposit facility delivered by the seller are to be made good by a cash payment.	Based on an average, less 0.25% of the offer rates to prime banking names stated by a random sample of designated banks taken between 9.30 a.m. and 11.00 a.m. on the last trading day. The settlement price will be 100.00 minus the rate thus obtained. Differences between the settlement rate and the actual rate on the deposit facility delivered by the seller are to be made good by a cash payment.	The LIFFE market price at 11.00 a.m. on the second business day prior to delivery. The invoicing amount in respect of each deliverable stock is to be calculated by the price factor system. The price factors are calculated by the Exchange and announced before trading for the relevant contract month has commenced. Adjustment will then be made for income accruing up to the delivery day.	The LIFFE official closing price on the last trading day. The Clearing House will pay interest on cleared U.S. dollar funds during the delivery cycle.
TRADING HOURS	8.30 a.m. to 3.00 p.m.	9.00 a.m. to 3.02 p.m.	9.30 a.m. to 3.15 p.m.	8.35a.m. 8.40a.m. 8.45a.m. 8.30a.m. to to to to 3.02p.m. 3.04p.m. 3.06p.m. 3.00p.m.

conventional cash market operators creates initial problems of familiarisation.

All four currency contracts are quoted against the US dollar, and are also QUOTED IN DOLLAR TERMS, that is, dollars per unit of the currency concerned (or, in the case of the yen, dollars per 100 yen). For instance, the quotes on a given day might look as follows:

GBP contract, quoted as   1·5625 ($/GBP)
DEM contract, quoted as 0·4051 ($/DEM)
CHF contract, quoted as 0·4854 ($/CHF)
JPY contract, quoted as   0·4260 ($/100 JPY)

The exchange lays down a minimum price interval at which price quotes may be made. In the case of the sterling contract this is 0·05 cents. Accordingly, if the price is now 1·5625, the next price quoted must be either 1·5630 or 1·5620. A price of 1·5627 would not be acceptable as a price on the exchange as it does not conform to the minimum price interval or 'tick' of 0·05 cents.

The cash value of a one tick movement on one sterling contract may be calculated thus:

GBP $25,000 \times 0·05 = \$12·50$ per contract

The contract sizes and tick sizes of the other exchange rate based contracts also give rise to a tick value of $12·50 per contract.

The two interest rate contracts are quoted on the basis of an index. The price is quoted as '100 – yield'. So, if the interest rate is, say, 11%, then the contract would be quoted as $100 - 11 = 89$. The purpose of this convention is to ensure that the contract behaves like a CD or a bill, so that its price will rise if rates fall. It is important to be aware of the definition of 'interest rate' used in pricing the contract. In the case of both these contracts this is 0·25% below the average offered price in the cash market, NOT LIBOR (London Interbank Offered Rate).

The tick size for the eurodollar contract is 1 basis point, or 0·01% per annum. This is equivalent to a tick value of $25, calculated thus:

$\$1,000,000 \times \frac{3}{12} \times 0·01/100 = \$25$

Similarly the tick size for the 3 month sterling contract is also one basis point and gives rise to a tick value of GBP 6.25. It is important to realise that the 3 month rate quoted is for a 3 month period commencing on the delivery date. Thus, if it is now February, a 3 month contract with a June delivery relates to an interest rate to apply from June to September. The calculation of rates for future periods is shown on p. 83. Note particularly that a rate of 15% in the 3 month period and of 15% in the 6 month period does NOT mean that the second 3 months is worth 15% too.

The gilt contract is quoted in the same way as an actual 20 year 12% gilt would be quoted in the cash market. That is, if current redemption yields were 12% then the contract would be quoted at 100, and if rates rose to 15% then it would be quoted at $81\frac{3}{32}$ on the cash market (as calculated from standard bond redemption yield tables), or 81–03 on the LIFFE convention, where the last two digits refer to $\frac{1}{32}$nds. For the GBP 50,000 contract size and $\frac{1}{32}$ tick size, the value of one tick is GBP 15·625.

Whereas there is no particular complexity arising in the quoting or trading of the gilt contract, complexities do arise if the contract is taken through to delivery date. Under the terms of the gilt contract any straight gilt with a first redemption date between 15 and 25 years out may be delivered in settlement. (But not variable rate, index linked, partly paid, or convertibles.) Since stocks with different coupons and maturities command different prices, a Price Factor for each deliverable gilt is calculated by the exchange which determines the amount due in settlement of the futures contract. Current price factor tables are obtainable from LIFFE for this purpose. Experience to date is that the cheapest deliverable stock is likely to be one of the stocks with the highest coupons.

7.5   Margin Requirements and Margin Accounts

Whenever a member trades on the exchange he is required to put up a deposit called 'Initial Margin' to the clearing house on a standard scale set by the clearing house. As explained above, when discussing the rôle of the clearing house, the purpose of the margin is to protect the clearing house against possible adverse price movements in the contract concerned. Accordingly, Initial Margin is set based on the volatility of the contract and represents an estimate of one day's movement in the contract value. Typically, Initial Margin is set at around 0·1% to 3·0% of the contract value.

For instance, if a member does one contract as buyer or seller in the $1 m eurodollar contract he will be required to put up $1000 to the clearing house. If the member is doing the transaction on behalf of an outside customer, he is also required by the exchange to take a deposit from his customer at least as large as this Initial Margin, so that the

PRICE DETERMINATION

1. BASED ON IMPLIED FUTURE RATE

    Euro $ 3 Month : 15%

    Euro $ 6 Month : 15%

   $100 Over 6 Months ⟶ $107.50

    "   " 3 " ⟶ $103.75

_____

But $103.75 earns $3.75 over second
3 months at only

       = 14.46%

         Implied Future Rate

2. QUOTED AS AN INDEX

        100 - yield

      = 85.54

risk is covered by margin throughout the dealing chain. The Initial Margin is repaid when the deal is closed out, either when doing an equal and opposite trade on a later date, or by reason of the deal maturing.

It is a feature of futures markets generally that unrealised gain and loss on the value of contracts outstanding is paid daily between the member and the clearing house. Thus, if a member has a contract whereby he bought one eurodollar contract at a price of 89, and the price today at close of business is 88, he has lost 100 ticks at $25 a tick, or $2500. He will therefore have to pay the clearing house $2500 in 'Variation Margin' to cover this unrealised loss. This sum of money will be in addition to the Initial Margin of $1000 paid up earlier on.

At this point the $2500 only covers the loss up to the close of business last night; any further loss arising today should in principle be covered by the Initial Margin. Variation Margin payments serve to keep the Initial Margin intact to meet possible adverse movements today. Variation Margin works in both directions; if losses must be paid in, gains are paid out. In the original example let us now suppose that the price had moved up to 90, giving him an unrealised gain of $2500. The clearing house would pay him $2500 in Variation Margin and his position would be:

> Initial Margin Paid ($1000)
> Variation Margin Rec'd $2500
> Net credit balance $1500

This daily settlement process ensures that price movements are directly reflected in cash movements – positions are automatically 'marked to market' every day. In turn, the member will debit or credit his customer daily for Variation Margin on his transactions, so that when a member deals on behalf of a customer, the margin payments simply pass between the clearing house and the ultimate customer via the member firm.

For most corporate customers these daily transfers of funds are an administrative inconvenience and so normally the customer will arrange with the member through whom he deals to set up a Futures Margin Account. This will usually be set up on the method known as the Maintenance Margin system. This is really no more complex than a simple current account with an agreed minimum balance called the Maintenance Balance. The customer opens the account with an Initial Balance of perhaps twice the Maintenance Balance (for instance the account may operate with an Initial Balance of $100,000 and a

DEALING AND MARGIN ARRANGEMENTS

1. This document should be read in conjunction with the Customer Agreement and forms an attachment to that Agreement.

2. Unless and until expressly directed otherwise by you in writing and we have acknowledged such written direction, we are authorised to act upon receipt of oral or written instructions from any one or more persons whom you may nominate in writing.

3. Confirmation of trades, statements of accounts, margin calls and any other notices sent by us shall be conclusive and deemed acknowledged by you as correct unless you give to us written notice to the contrary within five days of our despatching such confirmations, statements, margin calls or other notices.

4. Communications may be made to you at the address set opposite your name below or at such other address as you may hereafter give us in writing. All communications so made, whether by post, telex, cable, telephone, messenger or otherwise shall be deemed to have been given to you 24 hours after despatch whether actually received or not.

5. (Name of Member) shall not be responsible for delays in the transmission of orders due to breakdown, or failure of transmission, or communication facilities, or to any other cause beyond (Member's) control.

6. We shall have total discretion at all times as to whether we enter into any contract with you and shall not be required to give any reason for not entering into any proposed contract.

7. Member shall open a Futures Margin Account for you, either in US dollars for Eurodollar and Currency contracts or in Sterling for the Short Sterling and Long Gilt contracts, as appropriate.

8. The Initial Balance on your Futures Margin Account and the minimum or Maintenance Balance will be as set out on the attached Schedule of Margins and Commissions.

9 If the actual balance falls below the Maintenance Balance due to debits arising from Commission, Initial Margin, Variation Margin payments or otherwise, then you are required to restore the balance to at least the Initial Balance immediately. Attention is drawn to Clause 8(d) of the Customer Agreement.

10. Commission is payable on each contract taken out at rates set out on the attached Schedule of Margins and Commissions. The commission is for a round turn and includes the 'closing out' of the transaction subsequently, and is due and payable on the date when contracts are closed out, at latest on the delivery date. Commission will be charged by debit to your Futures Margin Account with ourselves.

11. Initial Margin is payable on each contract taken out on the day after the deal is done. The amount of Initial Margin required is set out on the attached Schedule of Margins and Commissions. Initial Margin will be charged by debit to your Futures Margin Account with ourselves.

12. As prices fluctuate each day, the value of outstanding contracts will change. The amount of unrealised gain (or loss) – Variation Margin – will be added to (or subtracted from) your Futures Margin Account with ourselves.

13. Debits and credits to Futures Margin Accounts arising from these arrangements will be made by ourselves as required, without further reference.

Maintenance Balance of $50,000). Thereafter the account is debited or credited for daily Variation Margin, Initial Margin, realised gains and losses, commissions, etc., on an automatic basis.

No payments from the customer are required unless the account balance falls below the Maintenance Balance, in which case the customer is required to top up the account to the Initial Balance once more. The customer is only involved in making or receiving actual payments relatively infrequently, the day to day movements on the account being otherwise automatically made by the member through whom he is dealing.

There is no dealer's turn or price margin in financial futures dealing. The price the treasurer gets is the price at which the deal was struck in the pit, and the buyer's price is identical to the seller's price. It follows that it is not possible to bargain for keener prices as perhaps would be the case in cash market foreign exchange or eurodollar dealing, nor is it possible to seek 'quantity discounts' and the like since all contract sizes are identical. Where, then, are the costs in using the market?

Costs arise in two ways. Firstly, and perhaps most obviously, members charge a commission per contract dealt, bought or sold. The commission relates to the 'round trip', covering both entering into the contract and its ultimate closing out. Commission is payable when the position is closed out, or upon delivery date if delivery takes place. Secondly, the funds put up as margin represent a cost, (whether as an actual expense or as an opportunity cost), and this cost is usually far more significant than the small sums typically charged as commission.

7.6   Customer Agreements

There are a number of formalities that the company must comply with prior to being in a position where the treasurer can simply phone up and deal through his member. Firstly there should be an agreement between the customer and the member as to the terms and conditions under which they should deal. This will cover the commissions to be paid, levels of margin, opening a Futures Margin Account, and the terms concerning interest if any to be paid on credit balances. The Terms and Conditions document essentially determines the cost of doing business on the exchange.

A second, more formal document, known as the Customer Agreement, is required by the exchange to be signed by every customer prior to doing any LIFFE transactions through a member. The Customer Agreement, of which a typical example appears on pp. 88–89, contains a standard clause warning would-be customers of the possibility of loss arising from contracts entered into, and also lays down LIFFE's rights to supervise the exchange and to intervene in the event of disputes. The customer also agrees to abide by the rules of the exchange in the handling of its transactions. In the agreement shown there are nine clauses, of which all, save only clause 8, are required by LIFFE to be in all Customer Agreements.

The Customer Agreements of certain members may include many additional clauses over and above those shown and may go on to cover aspects such as the operation of margin and the procedure for actual trades. These latter aspects are, however, more usually covered by a separate document on the lines of that shown headed 'Dealing and Margin Arrangements', which, as will be seen, covers the more day to day operational matters.

There is usually a fourth document in the form of a mandate, which takes the form of a letter to the member from the company formally requesting that a financial futures dealing relationship be opened and requesting that instructions relating to financial futures transactions be accepted by the member from designated, named officials of the company. In summary, then, the documentation to be completed prior to doing any futures transactions is likely to consist of:

a: Terms and Conditions

b: Customer Agreement

c: Dealing & Margin Agreement

d: Mandate

7.7 Placing an Order

Assuming that all the above formalities are now in order, and that the treasurer wishes to place an order to buy or sell with the member firm he has chosen, the actual procedure will be on the following lines.

The treasurer will phone the City office of the firm concerned, which is likely to have a specialist LIFFE Customer Desk, and enquire as to current market rates. If satisfied with the levels, he will leave an order with the Desk for execution. The Customer Desk will have a direct line to the firm's booth and the order will be called down to the booth man who records the order on a slip and sends it by

CUSTOMER AGREEMENT

The London International Financial Futures Exchange ("the Exchange")

Dear Sirs,

We refer to the arrangements under discussion between us for the purchase and sale of financial futures on the Exchange. Such arrangements shall be subject to the margin requirements, commissions, liquidation entitlements and other terms and conditions which already have been or may from time to time hereafter be agreed between us ("the Terms and Conditions"). Notwithstanding this, the following is expressly drawn to your attention:—

1. The object of the Exchange is to provide facilities for members and their clients to hedge against the risk of future changes in interest rates and foreign currency rates of exchange and such other risks as may be the subject of contracts traded on the Exchange. Notwithstanding this purpose, transactions in financial futures involve a risk of loss which may be substantial, and before entering into financial futures' contracts you must satisfy yourselves that such contracts are suitable for your purpose in every way and that their size is appropriate to your resources. You must rely on your own judgment in entering into such contracts. We do not hold ourselves (or any of our employees or agents) as having authority to advise you in connection with those contracts or financial futures generally and we accept no responsibility for any losses suffered by you as a direct or indirect result of the same.

2. You should be aware that under certain conditions, as for example when the market makes a "limit move", it may prove impossible to liquidate a position. Further, placing contingent orders, such as a "stop-loss" or "stop-limit" order, will not necessarily limit your losses to the intended amounts, since market conditions may make it impossible to execute such orders.

3. All contracts made on the Exchange and all transactions between us relating thereto shall be subject to the provisions of the Memorandum and Articles of Association of London International Financial Futures Exchange Limited ("LIFFE") and the rules of LIFFE and the general regulations of International Commodities Clearing House Limited ("ICCH") so far as the same are applicable and to the other terms and conditions agreed between us which are referred to above.

4. No benefit of any guarantee given by ICCH in respect of registered contracts shall extend to you unless you are a clearing member of LIFFE and of ICCH and such contracts are registered with ICCH in your name. All contracts between us for the purchase or sale of any security currency or other property are on the clear understanding that both of us contemplate actual delivery and other contracts between us subject to the rules of LIFFE contemplate actual performance.

5. In respect of every contract made between us subject to the rules of LIFFE we will have made or placed an equivalent contract or contracts on the floor of LIFFE for execution by open outcry and we shall thus have an interest in the transaction. Our contract note submitted to you will show the price at which the equivalent contract(s) has/have been executed on the floor.

6. Where ICCH does not allocate open long contracts on maturity direct to specific own account or customer account short contracts, or vice versa, we will normally allocate such contracts among our customers, including yourselves, on a first-in first-out basis, but in our discretion, if we consider it equitable, we may use such alternative basis of allocation (approved by LIFFE) as we may from time to time notify you.

7. Under the rules of LIFFE we may be required to disclose to officials of LIFFE's market supervision department particulars of our dealings with you under those rules including particulars of payment of sums by way of margin. By accepting this letter in the manner prescribed below, we shall have your authority to make any such disclosure. LIFFE has undertaken that all such information will remain confidential.

8. To the extent that the Terms and Conditions defined above conflict with the provisions of this letter then the latter shall prevail.
   In particular:—

   (a) you agree to indemnify and hold us harmless against and from all and any losses costs and/or damages (including costs and legal fees incurred in collecting such deficit) sustained by us resulting directly or indirectly from any act or omission by you with respect to contracts entered into and/or your accounts with us including, but not limited to, any deficit balances which may occur in the said accounts however arising;

   (b) you shall reimburse us, on demand, for all taxes imposts, duties and levies whatsoever charged upon us in connection with or in any way relating to your financial futures contracts (other than corporation tax on our profits or income);

   (c) all monies securities negotiable instruments open positions in financial futures contracts or other property of yours at any time including funds deposited to meet deposit and margin requirements or otherwise held by us may be sold, utilised and/or applied by us, without notice, in or towards satisfaction of all or any obligations or liabilities of yours to us; and

   (d) in the event of your failing to pay to us any sum when due (whether by way of margin, deficit balance or otherwise) we have the right to liquidate your position with us immediately without further notice.

9. Any dispute arising from or relating to this arrangement or any contract made hereunder shall, unless resolved between us, be referred to arbitration under the arbitration rules of LIFFE before either of us resort to the jurisdiction of the courts. Subject to this provision, disputes arising herefrom or from contracts made under the provisions of this arrangement shall be subject to the jurisdiction of the English courts, to which both parties hereby submit.

runner to the pit trader. The trader finds a counterparty for the deal, deals, and sends the runner back to the booth with the details of the deal done, including the price at which it was dealt. The booth man relays this back to the Desk, who phone the treasurer to advise that the contracts have been done and at what price. Margin is then debited to the customer's account and a statement of his current outstanding contracts, current account balance, and current position are sent by mail.

SELF TEST QUESTIONS

1 Using cash market foreign exchange and interest rates from Table A on p. xii, (and assuming that the LIFFE March delivery date is the same as the 3 month date), calculate the equivalent LIFFE market prices for March delivery for:

    a: sterling exchange rate contract

    b: deutschemark exchange rate contract

    c: 3 month eurodollar contract

        Hint: remember eurodollar contract based on 0.25% below the cash market offered rate.

2 Why do the rates calculated above differ from those shown as the LIFFE quotes for that day?

3 A company has a Futures Margin Account with its broker, and his position on a given day is:

        Balance on account $57,856
        Maintenance balance $50,000
        Initial balance $75,000

The company has existing contracts where it has bought 20 March eurodollar contracts at 92·00. Last night's settlement price at which variation margin has been calculated and debited to the account was 91·36. The company now sells 30 March eurodollar contracts at 91·12 and also sells 15 June deutschemark contracts at 0·4296. Commission is $28 per contract and initial margin for any contract is $1000 per contract.

a: What will the balance on the Futures Margin Account now become?

b: Will the company have to pay in additional funds to the broker, and if so, how much?

Answers

1 *a*: sterling exchange rate
middle forward price $= 1.62725 - 0.0047 = 1.62265$
to nearest 'tick' $= 1.6225$

b: deutschemark exchange rate
middle forward price $= 2.35655 - 0.0185 = 2.33805$
expressed as a reciprocal $= 0.4277068$
to nearest 'tick' $= 0.4277$

c: eurodollar
From the rates table the offered rates are:
eurodollar 3 month $9\frac{1}{8}\%$pa
eurodollar 6 month $9\frac{5}{16}\%$pa
But LIFFE settlement prices are reckoned on the basis of 0.25% below these offered rates, ie:
3 month $8\frac{7}{8}$
6 month $9\frac{1}{16}$
The March eurodollar contract relates to the 3 month period commencing in March, so the next step is to calculate this rate.

Interest on \$1m for 3 months at $8\frac{7}{8}\%$ is   \$22,187·50
Interest on \$1m for 6 months at $9\frac{1}{16}$ is   \$45,312·50
Thus, interest due to second 3 months is   \$23,125·00

This sum has to be earned on the maturing proceeds of the first 3 month deposit, being \$1,022,187 50. The interest rate required to do this is given by:
$$1,022,187·50 \times \tfrac{3}{12} \times R/100 = 23,125·00$$
which proves $R = 9·0492\%$ pa.

Quoting this rate as an index and then rounding to the nearest 'tick' then provides Price $= 100 - R = 90·95$

2 *a*: Arbitrage between cash and futures is not cost free, due to commissions, cost of margin on the futures side, and due to the price spread on the cash side of the arbitrage. Price gaps equal to the cost of arbitrage are thus able to persist.

b: Nevertheless, cash and futures seldom line up even that accurately in practice and arbitrage opportunities such as suggested by these small price differences are a normal feature of the market.

c: Some of the price gap is due to the fact that the dates are not the same; 3 months over spot takes us into April, the LIFFE date was 9 March.

d: It is unlikely that all these prices were taken out of the market at the same moment in the day; some of the apparent gap may be due to differences in the timing of the data gathering during the trading day.

3 Starting balance on account	$57,856

Re close out of 20 March eurodollars

Return of initial margin	$20,000
Commission, $28 × 20 contracts	($560)
Return of variation margin (92 − 91.36)	$32,000
Loss on sale (92 − 91·12)	($44,000)

Re sale of 10 March eurodollars

Initial margin	($10,000)

Re sale of 15 deutschemarks

Initial margin	($15,000)
Net balance at close	$40,296

below maintenance balance

Call from company required to take balance up to a minimum of $75,000; say $35,000 to be called.

8 Using Futures for Trading

8.1 Advantages of Futures Markets

All financial markets, if they are to grow and prosper, must establish for themselves a special niche amongst the wide range of existing services where they can offer particular advantages to their users. Financial futures markets, as relatively new arrivals within an already complex and sophisticated array of financial services, were required to have a number of advantages in their chosen field over the services already available. These advantages may be roughly thought of as:

a: those concerning financial futures generally

b: those mainly relevant to currency futures

c: those mainly relevant to interest rate futures

a) Concerning Financial Futures Generally
Since all futures deals have the clearing house as the counterparty and the credit risk is handled by the margin system, dealing in futures markets does not consume credit lines (save for the cash required for margin). Where existing credit lines are small, either absolutely or relative to a large turnover, futures markets provide a means to continue to operate and to lay off risk.

Secondly, a trader can operate 'invisibly' in futures markets, since he will probably trade via a broker. It will be the broker's name that will be seen in the pit, not the customer's; further, the counterparty will always be the clearing house so that the customer's name is never seen by the market at all.

Unlike cash markets, where big traders will secure better dealing prices because of their market 'clout', in futures markets all deal at the same price. There is, after all, no spread between the buying and selling price, so the only dealing cost involved is commission. For this reason small traders can often get a cheaper deal in futures markets than in the equivalent cash market.

b) Advantages Concerning Currency Futures

For most large corporate users currency futures will be of little interest as a means of routine foreign exchange cover, since the interbank market is both cheaper and more flexible than futures. Contract sizes are also too small for many large corporate users. However, as suggested above, for the smaller corporate user or even a large private individual, the futures market may well be the cheapest way of covering foreign exchange risks. In many cases banks are reluctant to offer forward dealing facilities to such smaller traders and the futures market may thus become the only means available for them to lay off currency risk.

c) Advantages Concerning Interest Rate Futures

This is the main area where financial futures can show clear advantages over all other conventional markets. Not surprisingly then, interest rate futures normally make up over 80% of the total volume of financial futures trading. Here the argument moves on to a different level; it is not so much whether the service is marginally cheaper or dearer, or even more convenient, but whether other markets can provide a similar service at all. The function of the market in interest rate futures is to protect companies from the financial consequences of changes in interest rates, which is something either extremely difficult or impossible to achieve in any other way.

It is theoretically possible to protect a company against swings in short term interest rates by doing loans and deposits for different periods, thus locking up the rate for the difference in the period concerned. In practice, however, the impact upon the balance sheet and its implication for gearing rule this out. Worse still, borrowing for one period and depositing for another consumes lines of credit available to the company in a way that is not normally acceptable. (A further idea is that a company may agree a forward deposit with its bank, fixing a rate at which the company will deposit for 3 months fixed, say 2 months from today. Certainly it can, but it will not usually be able to call up in a few weeks time and cancel the deal, or use the method with any degree of operational flexibility.)

By contrast, using futures to lock in future interest rates does not impact upon the balance sheet, or gearing, or credit lines in any way.

Following this line of thought one step further, it should be noted that taking out interest rate futures, whilst it changes the interest rate risk experienced by the firm, it has no effect upon liquidity. The fact that these two hitherto inextricably interwoven variables of interest rate risk and liquidity risk can thus be separated out and so separately controlled is a powerful improvement in the ability of the treasurer to manage the company's financial exposures.

8.2   Disadvantages of Financial Futures Markets

Futures markets are, of course, not the answer to everything and there are a number of undoubted snags. Of these the greatest is probably still the fact that these markets are relatively unfamiliar to a number of people. Worse, futures markets have typically been introduced to them in very dramatised style by the press, where the articles often stress the speculative nature of many market participants and the perhaps offputtingly flamboyant style of the Chicago markets. This can all too easily create a climate of opinion to the effect that the market is somehow not quite respectable and that prudent and responsible companies would not wish to use it.

This attitude is extremely close to that prevalent in the early 1970s when companies were being urged to cover foreign exchange risks using forward foreign exchange contracts. It was then felt that to use forward markets was simply betting; clearly dangerous and speculative. Today that attitude in all but the most diehard of companies has almost disappeared. People seek to cover known exchange risk quite routinely and even have well established teams of people whose job is to decide whether or not to take cover on a particular occasion. The acceptance process may be a little faster in the case of futures, having as it were been through the process once with forward foreign exchange; nevertheless the similarities to the former foreign exchange market attitude are striking.

As was formerly the case in the foreign exchange markets, the missing but necessary step in the reasoning is to evaluate whether the likely costs associated with not using the market exceed the likely cost of using it. When this evaluation is made against today's background of volatile foreign exchange and interest rates, then the initial psychological difficulties rapidly fade away.

As explained in Chapter 7, the formalities of setting up an arrangement to deal in futures are undoubtedly more complex than setting up to deal in foreign exchange. There are a number of documents requiring signature and even Board resolutions, and quite a lot of information to absorb as to what the documents mean. This too inevitably causes a certain amount of inertia.

The third and major disadvantage to the new user is the system of margin which requires him to give reasonably continuous attention to ensuring that the account is topped up as required. Whereas in practice this turns out to be fairly simple to do, in prospect it is bound to seem complex and time consuming. Related to this aspect is the fact that the accounting and financial control aspects for a company dealing in futures are more complex than for the transactions they have hitherto been doing in the cash markets. Again, even this difficulty arises in two separate ways. Firstly, that the unfamiliarity with the topic of futures and the accounting required for it makes the thought seem somewhat daunting, plus the fact that it is indeed slightly more complex.

8.3   Cash/Futures Arbitrage

The three main uses of financial futures are arbitrage, trading and hedging. These we treat in turn. Perhaps the simplest type of arbitrage is that between cash and futures. We saw in the previous chapter that, using actual market rates, LIFFE prices as calculated from cash market rates were not identical to the actual prices at which the contracts were being traded on the exchange. To the extent that they are different there is scope for a profitable arbitrage between the cash and futures markets, buying in one market and selling in the other at a profit turn in the price. For example, in the questions at the end of the previous chapter it was seen that the cash market forward exchange rate to March was 1·6226, while the futures market rate was 1·6235. Theoretically, and ignoring transaction costs, it would have been possible to buy forward sterling in the forward market and sell it on the futures market and make a riskless profit of 9 points.

More sophisticated arbitrage possibilities also exist on LIFFE owing to the existence of 3 month interest rate contracts in both dollars and sterling. There are no less than four ways to arrive at a dollar/sterling exchange rate for a LIFFE settlement date:

   (i) cash market forward rate

   (ii) futures market forward rate

   (iii) forward rate as calculated from the spot rate and a forward premium reckoned from the cash market dollar and sterling interest rates

   (iv) forward rate as above, but with the premium calculated from the futures market implied interest rates for dollar and sterling

EXAMPLE

To illustrate the possibilities we will take rates from Table A on p. xii as follows to calculate the results under cases (ii) to (iv) above for the June delivery date, which for simplicity we will assume to be identical to the six month date. Result (i), not quoted in Table A, we will assume to be, say, 1·6185.

Cash Market

spot dollar/sterling	1·6273
6 month eurodollar	$9\frac{5}{16}$
6 month sterling	$10\frac{7}{16}$

Futures Market

dollar/sterling, March	1·6235
dollar/sterling, June	1·6235
Eurodollar 3 month, March	91·12
Sterling 3 month, March	90·45

(i) 1·6185 (given)

(iii) forward premium:

$(10\frac{7}{16} - 9\frac{5}{16})/100 \times \frac{6}{12} \times 1\cdot6273 = 0\cdot0092$

outright price $= 1\cdot6273 - \cdot0092 = 1\cdot6181$.

(iv) equivalent 3 month eurodollar rate from March to June is

$(100 - 91\cdot12) + 0\cdot25 = 9\cdot13\%$

equivalent 3 month sterling rate from March to June is

$(100 - 90\cdot45) + 0\cdot25 = 9\cdot80\%$

forward premium March to June is given by:

$(9\cdot80 - 9\cdot13)/100 \times \frac{3}{12} \times 1\cdot6235 = 0\cdot0027$

outright to March is 1·6235, so outright to June is

$1\cdot6235 - 0\cdot0027 = 1\cdot6208$.

The obvious differences between these four results represent arbitrage opportunities. Nor do the possibilities end there. The basic calculation is that the two interest rates and the forward exchange rate form a logical triangle; if you fix any two of them the third may be calculated. This is true of the three cash market entities, and also true of the three futures market entities. Or any one cash market entity and one futures market entity enable us to calculate where the third should stand in both the cash and futures market. And if they are not at exactly that level, then there is an arbitrage opportunity.

Some operators, using computer based systems, can keep continuous check on these various arbitrage possibilities. Clearly this rôle is a minor one in the context of the market as a whole, but it does tend to ensure that futures market prices do not get too far out of line from the underlying cash market prices to which they relate. Arbitrage activity has the effect of increasing the depth of the market. A large order which the market could not perhaps otherwise absorb without a major price shift will tend to be taken out against the cash market by arbitrageurs.

8.4 Outright Trading

Financial futures may be traded like any other market; traders buy when they think the price is low and sell when they think the price is high. Several forms of trading are practised, which principally differ in the time horizon of the different participants. 'Scalpers' trade in the pit and try to take advantage of very short term fluctuations in prices (measured in minutes) trading for profits of the order of a couple of ticks only. Such traders may do a very large turnover during the day, making very modest profits and losses but adding considerably to the depth of the market. 'Day traders' take a slightly longer view, as their name suggests, aiming to open and close their books in a trading day, finishing and starting with a nil position. They too contribute to the depth of the market.

Longer term traders, which include many outside companies, take up a particular long term position, long or short, in the expectation that over a period prices will move in their favour. Such longer term hedgers are indistinguishable in the market from hedgers.

For a trader in interest rate futures, buying a futures contract is equivalent to buying a CD or a bill at a price fixed now for delivery on a future date. It will be profitable if interest rates fall. Selling an interest rate future is equivalent to selling a CD or a bill and will be profitable if interest rates rise.

An example of a typical position taker's deal is shown below, handled using cash markets in Case A and using futures markets in Case B. The situation in both cases is that the trader believes that eurodollar rates will fall and seeks to profit from his forecast.

EURODOLLAR TRADER EXPECTING RATES TO FALL.   A
Deposit Market Operation Borrow 1 month @ 15% Lend   6 month @ 15¼% After one month Borrow 5 month @ 13%

Profit $9583
But:
    — Increases Balance Sheet
    — Uses up Credit Lines
    — Worsens Liquidity Ratios

Case A

In case A the trader lends $1m of 6 month money at the prevailing rate of $15\frac{1}{4}\%$ and takes in 1 month money against it at 15%. For the first month he will accrue a positive turn of $\frac{1}{4}\%$ per annum and he will hope to borrow again after one month at a lower rate in order to continue to accrue a profit.

Let us suppose that his forecast is correct and that after one month has elapsed he is able to borrow for the next 5 months at 13%. The arithmetic is that he will secure an accrued profit of $9,583 as a result of this operation. But the trader faces a number of problems with this type of transaction:

   a: The balance sheet has been increased by $1m.

   b: The gearing is increased.

   c: His borrowing uses part of his credit lines.

   d: His lending also uses part of his own lending lines.

   e: For the first month, liquidity is impaired.

All of these problems are significant, and taken together may rate as sufficient deterrent to doing the deal that it is not carried out at all. These difficulties can be avoided by using the futures market as shown in Case B.

EURODOLLAR TRADER EXPECTING RATES TO FALL.   B
Futures Market Operation Buy 1 month @ 85·04 Buy 4 month @ 84·59 After one month Cover Spot @ 87·00 Sell 3 month @ 87·24
Profit = (196 + 265) × \$25   = \$11,525

Case B

Here, in exactly the same situation, the trader expecting rates to fall and therefore futures prices to rise, will buy a \$1m contract for the 1 month date and a further \$1m contract for the 4 month date. After 1 month has elapsed and interest rates have fallen to 13% his first contract will mature at a price of $(100 - 13) = 87$ and, let us suppose, the 3 month price has moved to 87·24. His profit, ignoring margin and commission costs, would be \$11,525. This profit is of a similar size to that earned in Case A, but it is not identical. The difference arises in a number of ways.

Firstly, it is only possible to get futures contracts spaced three months apart because that is how the delivery months are set. To hedge a four or five month gap directly is not possible on the present system of quarterly delivery dates. It should be further observed that if our example were not a straight speculation but was in fact a hedge against some other part of the company's cash flow, the company might wish to hedge for an amount other than a multiple of \$1m. Since eurodollar futures contracts are only available in multiples of \$1m this too creates an inflexibility, resulting in an inexact hedge.

There is a further and more fundamental reason why the futures outturn does not exactly mirror the cash market outturn. It is that at any time there exists a difference between futures prices and their underlying cash market prices, and that this 'basis' is not necessarily constant over time.

As a totally different example of a trader using futures we may consider a Gilt trader, who has a running portfolio of Gilts of a certain size, but trades the market in and out varying the size of his book according to his short term view of the market. Such a trader may well find it cheaper to keep his portfolio of actual Gilts static, but trade in and out with futures, thereby saving stockbroker's commissions. Taking this one step further, if the trader became bearish he could even sell Gilts futures to an extent that would cause his total book of actual + futures to be negative, a tactic not possible without the use of futures.

The above trades were simple outright positions. In the eurodollar example, if interest rates went down futures would go up and the trader would make money. Equally it was a high risk trade, in that the reverse could easily occur, giving rise to a loss. A lower risk technique is 'Spread Trading'.

8.5 Spread and Straddle Trading

Spread traders operate by simultaneously buying and selling two different but related contracts, for instance buying the DM contract and selling the Swiss franc contract, looking to turn a profit on a change in the differential between the two contracts. A spread trader forms a view as to the size of differential that he considers 'normal' between two contracts and trades in the market when the differential moves away from this level. For the trader to have a reasonable chance of success the two contracts involved should be related:

e.g.: LIFFE eurodollar v IMM 90 day T Bill
or LIFFE DEM   v LIFFE CHF

In the first of these pairs, both contracts would go up if rates fell (although probably by different amounts); in the second pair both contracts would go up if the dollar were weak in the exchange markets (although again probably by different amounts). Accordingly, a spread trader is incurring a lower degree of risk per contract than the outright trader. Spread traders, piqued by the occasional jibe concerning cowardice from supposedly red-blooded outright traders, are likely to point out that they compensate by doing many more contracts. From which it may been seen that this type of spread trading is not an activity likely to have much appeal to the average treasurer; it should be regarded as simply another way to assist market depth and ensure that price distortions do not persist.

But one type of spread trade is of considerable practical

importance, the spread between two different months in the same contract, known as a 'straddle'.

e.g   Buy 10 Dec eurodollar at 91·12 (yield = 8·88%)
      Sell 10 Mar eurodollar at 90·76 (yield = 9·24%)

Margin requirements are reduced for straddles; LIFFE initial margin on each pair of contracts forming a straddle is the same as the initial margin on a single contract of the same type. The straddle trade above would be referred to as 'buying the spread', the buy or sell referring to the near date transaction. The value of the spread is the near date price minus the far date price:

$$91·12 - 90·76 = 0·36 = 36 \text{ basis points.}$$

The effect of this straddle is to take a view on the slope of the yield curve, rather than on the absolute level of interest rates. Buying the spread implies a view that the difference between the December price and the March price will increase, or that the yield curve will steepen.

Let us work through the implications of this transaction with various possible outcomes. The initial position is that the futures prices imply yields of 8·88% for December 3 month dollars and 9·24% for March 3 month dollars.

3 month rate to commence	DEC	MAR
Start	8·88	9·24
Case A	9·14	9·73
Case B	9·14	9·26
Case C	9·88	10·24

(Diagrams depict 'Start' and 'Case A'.)

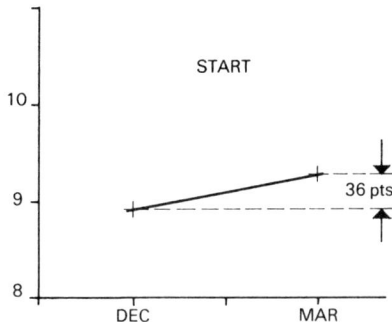

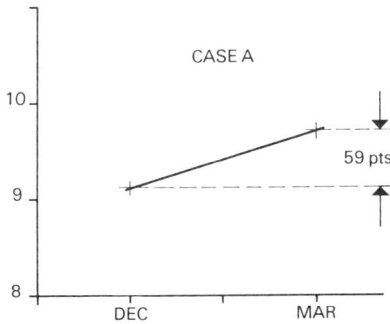

In Case A the spread moves up to 59 basis points and the spread can be sold with a gain of 23 basis points. In Case B, although interest rates rise, the spread actually falls, to 12 basis points, causing a loss of 24 basis points. In Case C, interest rates rise but the spread is unchanged, remaining at 36 basis points; the trade breaks even.

Straddles in currency contracts are directly comparable with swap prices in the forward foreign exchange market. As an example, rates in the two markets on 9 August 1983 for dollar/sterling were:

	Futures		Cash (FX market)
Sep	1·4931		1·4930
Dec	1·4955		1·4955
Mar	1·4980		1·4977
straddle Sep/Dec	24 pts	swap Sep/Dec	25 pts
straddle Dec/Mar	25 pts	swap Dec/Mar	22 pts

As is apparent, disparities between the two markets were very small, with no room for profitable arbitrage if costs are taken into account.

9 Using LIFFE for Hedging

9.1 Hedging Transactions

Hedging is an operation designed to reduce, ideally to zero, some existing risk. In principle a treasurer could use LIFFE to hedge either foreign exchange or interest rate risk, but in most cases foreign exchange risk will be more economically handled in the interbank forward markets. This chapter will therefore be concerned with the use of LIFFE contracts to hedge interest rate risk.

Any organisation whose results could be adversely affected by a change in interest rates is a potential hedger. The essential feature is that the risk arises in the business anyway, and that the futures transaction is used to reduce that risk.

Traders in futures markets must obviously rely on changes in futures prices to make their profits and must be aware that these will not necessarily move in line with the changes occurring in the underlying cash markets. Those using futures markets to hedge cash positions cannot thereby exactly eliminate their risk as they remain vulnerable to any change in the 'basis' between cash and futures. It is a truism of futures hedges that they convert outright risk of rate changes into the lesser basis risk. It is for this reason that professional futures hedgers spend so much time and effort in analysing the variability of basis over time.

There will, for instance, be times when futures prices start to discount expected changes in the cash market and, therefore, basis will alter. If subsequently the cash market rates do change, for instance due to a discount rate or base rate change, then the cash market price will move rapidly whereas the futures market will have already made part of the move in advance. Basis will tend to return to near its former level.

Whether to Hedge
Although basis risk is not zero, and the hedge is therefore always going to be somewhat imperfect, basis risks are of a smaller order of magnitude than the original outright risk. The fact that the hedge cannot be perfect should not distract one from the basic proposition, which is:

Is hedging likely to be cheaper than not hedging?

If the answer to this is 'yes', then hedge! But what if the answer is 'maybe', or even 'no'? No business could afford to run an unlimited interest rate risk even if it were felt at the time that rates would move in its favour. The level of risk has to be limited in some way and managed within the set limit. A hedging policy should contain the following ingredients if it is to be systematically pursued:

a: Identify present exposure to interest rate risk. One simple way to measure this is to calculate the effect on the profit and loss account of a 1% adverse change in interest rates.

b: Establish the maximum acceptable level of this risk, say X thousand pounds.

c: Hedge down to this level irrespective of the outlook for interest rates.

d: Regularly evaluate whether the expected direction of interest rate movements will be adverse to the company, and with what degree of confidence that opinion is held. On the basis of the view held, decide what percentage of the X thousand pounds maximum position to hedge at any given time.

e: If deciding to hedge, decide on the most appropriate hedging instrument and the number of contracts required.

f: Keep decisions (*d*) and (*e*) above under review.

g: Be aware that a hedge, although effective in offsetting loss if rates move as expected, will also offset any profit that will arise if rates move the other way.

9.2 Interest Risk and Liquidity

It was noted when looking at the particular advantages of futures markets in **8.1** on p. 93 that interest rate futures change interest rate risk but do not impact upon liquidity. This contrasts with all cash market instruments where, for example, placing a fixed deposit changes interest rate risk but also changes liquidity. The fact that the two variables of interest risk and liquidity can be separated out by using futures enables them to be controlled separately. This represents a major step forward in the treasurer's ability to control the company's risks.

This aspect can perhaps be most easily visualised by considering the situation of a bank deposit dealer. He will have a target of his desired liquidity profile (that is, the ideal maturity pattern of his loans and deposits from the point of view of prudent liquid resources to meet withdrawals, defaults and contingencies), but he will also have his view as to the likely future course of interest rates and, within limits, will wish to set up his book of maturities to accord with this view. It is clearly possible that the ideal maturity pattern from the liquidity point of view may be totally different from that ideal in terms of his market view as to interest rates. Indeed, Murphy's Law ensures that this is nearly always the case. Prior to futures markets the usual 'solution' was a sort of woolly compromise; to set up a maturity profile that was not unacceptably bad from either point of view, but which clearly far from optimised either liquidity or interest risk.

Today it is possible to set up the 'ideal' book from the point of view of liquidity and then examine the resultant interest rate risk. If that risk is not acceptable, or even if it deviates only slightly from where the dealer would ideally like it to be, he can take out futures contracts to fine tune the interest rate risk, without altering his carefully constructed liquidity profile.

EXAMPLE

A bank takes a deposit of GBP 3m for 3 months fixed at 10%. Wishing to improve liquidity at the time, the bank lends the funds for 1 month fixed at $9\frac{1}{2}\%$. Clearly the bank faces a loss accrual of $\frac{1}{2}\%$, but this has to be accepted as the market 'cost of liquidity'. The real problem is that, if rates generally fall, then the return on the funds in months 2 and 3 will be substantially below the $9\frac{1}{2}\%$ obtained during month 1, although the funds will continue to cost 10%. This risk may be hedged with futures. It is December, and March 3 month sterling interest rate futures stand at 90·73 (i.e. 9·27%).

First calculate the number of contracts required to hedge. There is a 2 month exposure on GBP 3m, which may be thought of as 6 'million pound months':

GBP 3m × 2 months = 6 'million pound months'

Sterling contracts on LIFFE are for GBP 0·25m per contract, and each contract runs for 3 months. Each contract thus covers $3 \times 0\cdot25 = 0\cdot75$ 'million pound months'.

No. of contracts required = 6/0·75 = 8 contracts.

The bank will lose money on its basic position if rates fall, so the hedge must make money if rates fall to compensate. Thus the bank must BUY futures to hedge. So the bank buys 8 sterling contracts at 90·73.

After 1 month
Suppose rates are now:

Cash 1 month	$8\frac{3}{4}\%$
Cash 3 month	9%
March futures	91·49 (i.e. 8·51%)

Renew interbank loan for a further month at $8\frac{3}{4}\%$. Accrual worsens by $\frac{3}{4}\%$ for the next month and will cost:

$$\tfrac{3}{4} \times \tfrac{1}{100} \times 3m \times \tfrac{1}{12} = GBP\ 1875$$

Remaining interest risk is GBP 3m for 1 month only, so that only 4 contracts are now required to achieve a hedge. Thus the bank now sells 4 contracts at 91·49 to give a gain of GBP 1900.

After 2 months
Suppose rates are now:

Cash 1 month	8%
Cash 3 months	$8\frac{3}{8}\%$
March futures	92·6 (i.e. 7·84%)

Renew loan for final month at 8%. Accrual is now worse by $1\frac{1}{2}\%$ versus month 1 and will cost:

$$1\cdot5 \times \tfrac{1}{100} \times 3m \times \tfrac{1}{12} = GBP\ 3750$$

But the four remaining contracts have a profit of 92·16 – 90·73 = 143 points/contract. These are now sold to realise a gain of $143 \times 4 \times GBP\ 6\cdot25/point = GBP\ 3575$.

Summary

Loss on accruals	$1875 + 3750 = (5625)$	
Gain on futures	$1900 + 3575 = 5475$	
Net G/(L)	(150)	
Hedge efficiency $= 5475/5625 \times 100\% =$	$97 \cdot 3\%$	

That is, $97 \cdot 3\%$ of the loss was protected by the futures hedge; the balance was caused by the change in the basis during the two months.

The example refers to sterling, but similar operations can equally well be conducted in dollars, or even (as we shall see in **9.5**) other currencies where LIFFE contracts do not exist.

9.3 Hedging Rollovers

Perhaps the most frequently used futures hedge is one designed to protect companies from a change in interest rate prior to a planned loan or deposit renewal – hedging a rollover.

Consider a company having a medium term eurodollar rollover loan, which is rolled over six-monthly with interest payable at an agreed margin over the six month LIBOR. Interest rates are thus locked up six months at a time and are fixed at whatever LIBOR happens to be on the rollover date. Suppose the company has a $15m loan with the next rollover currently 5 months away. Interest rates seem set to rise and the treasurer seeks to limit the impact upon his borrowing cost at the next renewal. For the hedge to work it must make money if interest rates rise; so he must SELL futures.

Arithmetic

6 month eurodollar LIBOR now (June)	13%
3 month eurodollar Dec contract	$86 \cdot 83$
3 month eurodollar Mar contract	$86 \cdot 40$

The period to be hedged is 6 months commencing November so the nearest fit is the 'strip' of contracts Dec and Mar. The treasurer sells:

15 Dec at $86 \cdot 83$
15 Mar at $86 \cdot 40$

At the November date the rates have become:

6 month eurodollar LIBOR	16%
3 month eurodollar Dec contract	$84 \cdot 10$
3 month eurodollar Mar contract	$83 \cdot 70$

Buy back the futures contracts, provides a gain of:

$$15 \times \$25/\text{point} \times (273 + 270) = \$203,625$$

Increased loan cost due to 3% rise in LIBOR:

$$\$15m \times \tfrac{3}{100} \times \tfrac{6}{12} = \$225,000$$

$$\text{Hedge efficiency} = 90 \cdot 5\%$$

A number of types of shorter term borrowing also behave like rollover credits from the interest risk point of view – whenever the borrowing is likely to be renewed on maturity. Sterling acceptance credits provide an example of this, where the short sterling contract provides an approximate means of hedging any adverse change in bill rates prior to renewal.

The question of rollover hedges can also be looked at from the point of view of a depositor who expects to renew a maturing deposit. He will seek to hedge against any fall in rates between now and his maturity date. Deposit hedgers BUY futures to achieve compensation for rate movements.

9.4   Charters and Projects

The viability of many projects and other business decisions may be critically dependent on the cost of money. A particular case in point is a ship charter transaction. A shipowner will typically have his major costs in operating the vessel as depreciation, finance, and fuel. Offered a charter fixture of $ X a month, one of the greatest factors influencing the viability of a charter at the proposed rate will be the cost of finance during the life of the charter. Other costs, although also variable in some degree, are likely to be relatively more stable. If the shipowner has financed his vessel with say, a rollover loan in dollars, he has the ability to use futures to hedge against any increase in the cost of finance during the life of the charter. By this means he is able to 'lock up' the net return on his charter within close limits and reduce the risk inherent in his decision.

Building and contracting companies face similar problems when estimating the cost of a construction project; the cost of finance until ultimate sale is not only a major element but also one of the factors most subject to variation. Construction companies can therefore sell futures to hedge against a rise in interest rates.

Many other such situations can easily be envisaged, the common thread is that if interest rates are a major element in the viability of a planned venture of any kind, then some of the business risk can be removed by using a futures hedge.

9.5   Hedging in Other Currencies

It may be reasonably supposed that interest rate hedges would only be possible in the two currencies, dollars and sterling, where interest rate futures contracts exist. All very useful no doubt, but what if the treasurer seeks to hedge against a shift in DEM interest rates? Or Swedish kronor?

This too can be handled if we recall the foreign exchange swap relationship, approximately expressed as:

Currency A forward premium per annum =
(eurodollar rate – currency A rate)/spot exchange rate

This formula is usually used from spot date, that is for instance, the forward premium between spot and the 3 month date is used with the 3 month eurodollar rate to calculate the 3 month interest rate for the currency concerned. But the same formula will also operate perfectly well for a future start date, and so can be used to derive 'futures prices' for any currency with an active forward foreign exchange market.

Eurodollar futures provide the eurodollar input and the cash forward FX market provides the swap price (being the forward premium between the start date and finish date of the futures contract). This establishes a futures price for the currency concerned which may be used for hedging. The example which follows shows how.

EXAMPLE

A company has a 3 month rollover loan in French francs of $ 1m equivalent. There are rumours that the currency may come under pressure in the near future (which does not help the treasurer as his loan is financing a French franc asset) and the company seeks to hedge against any sudden rise in French franc rates that could arise as a result of the exchange rate pressure. His next rollover is nearly 3 months ahead, in March.

Rates	in Dec	in Mar
spot FF/$	7·96	8·14
3 month premium, points	900	1750
6 month premium, points	2250	n/a
3 month FF LIBOR	15	$18\frac{3}{8}$
Mar eurodollar, LIFFE	89·96	90·14

Calculation
Swap price, 3m to 6m, $= (2250 - 900) = 1350$ points
Interest rate, premium over dollars:

$$1350/7·96 \times 12/3 \times \tfrac{1}{100} = 6·78\%$$

Implied futures rate for March eurofrancs:

$$89·96 - 6·78 = 83·18 \text{ (i.e. } 16·82\%)$$

Action
     Sell 1 Dec eurodollar contract at 89·96
     Buy the swap at 1350 points in the forward FX market

The objective is to protect against any worsening of the existing 16·82% rate for the period concerned.

In March
Swap price now is 1750 points
Interest premium over dollars is:

$$1750/8·14 \times 12/3 \times \tfrac{1}{100} = 8·60\%$$

Implied futures rate for eurofrancs:

$$90·14 - 8·60 = 81·54 \text{ (i.e. } 18·46\%)$$

Action
     Buy back the eurodollar at 90·14
     Sell the swap at 1750 points

Economics

Loss on eurodollar contract

$90\cdot14 - 89\cdot96 = 18$pt × \$25/pt	= \$ (450)
\$ cost of swap 1350 pts at $7\cdot96$	= \$(16,960)
\$ proceeds from swap, 1750 pts at $8\cdot14$	= \$ 21,499
Net gain on hedge	= \$ 4,089
Increased cost of loan ($18\cdot375\% - 16\cdot82\%$)	= \$ (3,888)
Hedge efficiency	= 105%

Notes

   (i) Although the actual 3 month rate from today as at the start of the hedge was 15% there is already nothing that can be done about the differential between this rate and the $16\cdot82\%$, since the $16\cdot82\%$ is the rate today for the 3 month period to commence in March.

  (ii) Hedge efficiencies can be greater or less than 100, according to whether they overshoot or undershoot. An efficiency of 105% is no 'better' than 95%; it is merely 5% off target in the opposite direction.

 (iii) The gain on the hedge could alternatively have been calculated as:

$(83\cdot18 - 81\cdot54) = 164$ pts × \$25/pt = \$4,100

The \$11 difference is simply a rounding error. The version shown in the example has the merit of showing the sources of the various components of the gain.

It is of course possible to construct similar implied interest rate contracts with currency futures contracts (as was shown in **8.5** on p. 101, a currency future straddle is equivalent to a foreign exchange swap), but:

   a: currency futures are only available in a few currencies.

   b: liquidity is poor.

   c: contract sizes do not correspond with the interest rate contracts, so that there are untidy 'loose ends'. For example, the DEM contract is DEM 125,000; if today's exchange rate is $2\cdot6460$ then we require $21\cdot168$ contracts to match one eurodollar contract!

9.6   Tailormade Hedges

We have already seen that futures markets do not track cash positions precisely, so that hedge efficiencies depart from 100%. We now examine the four main sources of these differences, and, where possible, suggest techniques for reducing them and improving accuracy. The problems are:

(i)   basis volatility

(ii)   convergence

(iii)   regression ratio on cross hedges

(iv)   bias due to variation margin

Basis Volatility

Cash/Futures basis volatility is simply the extent to which the basis between cash and futures changes over time. This volatility can be measured from historical price data so that the likely size of the variability is known in advance. If typical volatility can cause 3% shifts in hedge efficiency it may not matter very much; if 20%, then the hedger ought to be aware that his residual risk, despite the nominal hedge, is substantial. These variations in expected efficiency also provide a guide to the extent to which hedges will require to be monitored once in place.

Convergence

On the delivery date of a contract basis is likely to be at or very near to zero. Since the futures becomes the cash instrument on delivery, arbitrage will ensure that this occurs. It follows that, as a contract nears its delivery date, that basis will steadily move towards zero; this process is known as 'convergence'. Hedgers running a contract to delivery date should be aware that they will therefore experience a change in the basis to zero from the level existing at the date when they took out their hedge. This means that the expected change in the value of the futures contract will not exactly offset the change in value of the underlying cash position. Since the hedger knows both the direction and size of the change in the futures price due to convergence, he can allow for it when setting up his hedge by doing marginally more or less contracts.

Cross Hedges

Hedgers frequently require to hedge a position for which there is no direct futures counterpart. For instance:

- using LIFFE short sterling to hedge sterling acceptances
- using LIFFE 20 year Gilts to hedge a 7 year eurosterling bond
- using LIFFE 3 month eurodollar to hedge a 6 month rollover
- using LIFFE eurodollar to hedge a US T bill portfolio

In such cases it is unlikely that a 1% shift in interest rates will cause the same change in the cash value of the futures contract as in the underlying position being hedged. Sometimes this ratio can be obtained by straight calculation (or from tables in the case of Gilts of different coupons and maturities) but sometimes historical data must be used to determine the ratio by regression analysis. This information is then used to size the hedge.

EXAMPLE

Suppose a regression analysis shows that a 1% change in US T bill prices correlates with a 1·25% change in eurodollar futures prices. (That is, eurodollar prices are typically more sensitive than T bills and prices move further.) In order to cross hedge a $10m T bill portfolio with eurodollar futures, the best fit would not be 10 contracts but:

$$10/1 \cdot 25 = 8 \text{ contracts.}$$

Variation Margin

So far we have ignored variation margin in evaluating hedges, yet the effect of these cash flows on hedge efficiency can be substantial.

Normally a hedge is designed to counteract an anticipated loss in the underlying position, so that the futures contracts done to offset this are expected to make a profit. Again, normally the loss will be unrealised during the life of the hedge, whereas the futures gain will be paid out daily as variation margin to the hedger and is available for investment. The return on these funds biases the hedge so that the futures side of the hedge may be seen to have been set a little too high. 'Tailing' may be used to adjust the number of contracts so as to restore the hedge efficiency, by calculating the amount of opposite bias necessary to cancel out the above effect.

On the first day of the hedge variation margin is nil; on the last day we assume there is a gain of say $ G. On average then, during the life of the hedge our best guess of the size of the variation margin is $ G/2.

Also it should not be forgotten that the gain of \$ G is also available for a further 3 months after the hedge is closed out since interest in the cash market is not due until the loan matures (assuming a 3 month loan or deposit). Thus the total profit from the futures contract is:

$$G + G \times 91/360 \times R/100 + G/2 \times d/360 \times R/100$$
Where R = rate of interest on short term funds
d = no of days until hedge will be closed

The 'Tail Factor' is the ratio between this sum and the nominal gain G alone. The number of contracts required to achieve a hedge is the nominal number divided by the Tail Factor. Rearranging the sum above a little and dividing by G, we now get:

$$\text{Tail factor} = 1 + R/36000(91 + d/2)$$

EXAMPLE

Company has a \$65m 6 month eurodollar rollover loan to hedge with LIFFE 3 month contracts. Rollover date is 108 days distant when the hedge is considered, short term dollars earn $9\frac{1}{2}\%$, and the regression factor between 6 month and 3 month eurodollars is 1·07, with the 3 month rate the more volatile. How many contracts should be used to hedge?

$$\text{Tail factor} = 1 + 9\cdot5/36000(91 + 54) = 1\cdot0383$$
$$\text{No. of contracts} = 65/(1\cdot0383 \times 1\cdot07) = 58\cdot5$$
Say, use 58 contracts.

Hedge efficiency is kept under review during the life of the hedge to see whether or not this number of contracts is in fact providing a good match. Such a review might look as below:

Remaining life of hedge	64 days
Current no. of contracts	58
Current loss on underlying position	\$216,206
Current variation margin (gain)	\$226,604
Interest earned on variation	\$3,184
Hedge efficiency to date	106·3%
Hedge has run for	44 days

Tail factor for a hedge starting today:
(Short term rates now $10\frac{1}{8}\%$)

$$= 1 + 10\cdot125/36000(91 + 32) = 1\cdot0346$$

No. of contracts for a new hedge starting today would be:

$$65/(1.0346 \times 1.07) = 58.7$$

But on the 44 days to date it turns out that we have overhedged by 6·3%, and we should aim to recover this imbalance over the 64 days to run. This requires us to underhedge by $44/64 \times 6.3\% = 4.33\%$. So we should go for $58.7/1.0433 = 56.28$ contracts. At this point then the decision is to cut 2 contracts and run a hedge of 56 contracts until the next review.

Some hedgers attempt even finer tuning by allowing for the 0·28 of a contract indicated above by taking out 1 contract and running it for 28% of the time to run and then cutting. This is necessarily a little hit and miss as it relies for its success on prices moving in more or less a straight line over the full period so that they will pick up 28% of the price swing by holding the contract for 28% of the period. Many other hedgers operate as we have indicated above, dealing only to the nearest contract and ignoring fractions, but paying meticulously regular attention to the monitoring of the hedge efficiency during the life of the hedge and adjusting to suit.

9.7 Tax

At the outset of the new LIFFE market in 1982 the Inland Revenue, jointly with LIFFE, issued draft guidelines as to the tax treatment of LIFFE contracts. Although some areas were not clarified at this stage (such as the treatment for pension and life assurance funds and certain other special situations) the outline was reasonably clear as applied to the ordinary trading company. The brief summary below is necessarily broad brush and any user seeking definitive tax advice in their own particular situation should consult their usual professional advisers.

Trading in LIFFE contracts
Financial companies, traders in futures, and companies trading actively enough to be 'carrying on a trade' in futures will be assessed under Schedule D Case 1, gains and losses being treated as ordinary trading items. The Revenue will normally accept current mark to market recognition of gain and loss in line with market practice, so long as this is consistently applied.

Hedging

Hedging a trading situation, i.e. hedging a short term loan financing current inventories or receivables, will be treated as an ordinary trading expense or revenue and so also assessed under Schedule D Case 1.

Hedging a capital item, such as a long term loan or the purchase price of a capital asset, will be treated as part of the cost of the loan or asset concerned, so long as the hedge can be identified to the asset concerned. Gains will be liable to Capital Gains Tax rules and not treated as trading income.

Care should be exercised when considering a hedge of a capital nature in case the tax rate on the underlying situation is not the same as will apply to the futures hedge. It also should be checked that the tax position is truly symmetric so that gains and losses offset. If this is not the case then the hedge may have to be factored up or down in size to produce a neutral post tax effect.

10 Technical Forecasting

10.1 Economic Fundamentals

Traditional forecasting methods for exchange rates or interest rates rely on identifying economic variables that correlate reasonably well with market rates. The economic variable is then forecast using conventional economic analysis and then, assuming the correlation to hold, the derived rate is projected. For instance, it is now well established that over long term periods of perhaps ten years or so exchange rate changes tend to reflect the differential in the inflation rates between the two countries concerned. (This relationship held very well throughout the 1970s; as an example of the 22% appreciation of the DEM against the dollar in the years 1973–6 some 20% was accounted for by the inflation differential in favour of the DEM.)

Following the same line of approach, economists have developed 'models' to predict exchange rates from a whole range of economic criteria, including of course inflation rate but including many other variables as well, such as money supply growth rates, balance of payments measures, indices of economic growth and relative competitiveness in international trade and so on. Naturally, some of these models are more reliable than others, but assuming that they have been competently constructed they will normally provide a reasonable indication of the likely direction and size of medium term exchange rate movements.

But all forecasts based upon economic fundamentals suffer from the drawback that they are necessarily forecasts of trend lines. Actual rates fluctuate considerably from their underlying trend lines in the short term and can show substantial movements even day to day.

10.2 Limitations

Practical forecasts for treasury decisions are forced to concentrate on the shorter term, say 1, 3 or 6 months. Over such a time period a long term trend line for an exchange rate might only move perhaps 2%. For instance, if the French franc falls on average by 6% per annum relative to the Deutsche mark, then the trend line will fall $1\frac{1}{2}$% in a quarter. Which is only more or less a typical day's movement in today's markets and so not much use as a forecast. As has been discussed before, if rates typically move 20% a year, the fact that the trend line may move 6% may not seem too important. It is entirely possible to get the trend correct yet get all the short term movements wrong and so end up losing a lot of money. Regrettably, what matters to the treasurer is to forecast the volatility itself. But how?

Some forecasters and forecasting companies use an economic model like those discussed to set up basic trend line forecasts, then set out to identify where the currency is now relative to that trend line (e.g. '$ is now some 11% overvalued relative to its current equilibrium value . . .'). They then overlay this with other data, comment and opinion intended to provide an indication of the direction of the next move. That is, will the currency move further away from trend or commence its return towards it again?

Such 'kitchen sink' methods can be quite effective, and are certainly an improvement over 'pure' economic models. Aspects that may be taken into account by such kitchen sink forecasters include:

– market comment and dealers' opinions
– political comments
– behaviour of related markets, such as equities, bonds
– general economic data, such as GNP growth, industrial production, trade balance etc
– international and national political factors

Clearly the quality of this type of forecast is now heavily dependent upon the weight given to each of these factors by the forecaster, and becomes very subjective indeed.

A further limitation with all economic based methods is the

difficulty of assessing the timing of a forecast move. We 'know' that eventually the currency will come back to its trend line, but when? This month or next year? The kitchen sink method can provide some clues here, but the timing problem is still a serious one.

10.3   Introduction to Technical Methods

This shorter term area, where the economics based techniques start to let us down, is exactly where technical analysis or 'chartist' methods seem to come into their own. These concern themselves with the perennial human conflict between greed and fear in any market and with the characteristic price patterns seen in markets over time. Prices, after all, are made by people and their reactions stay pretty much the same over time.

Chartists seek to identify recurring patterns in price movements which suggest when a rise or fall may be reasonably expected. Technical analysis may be regarded as either pure mumbo – jumbo or as a mathematically based technique for quantifying learning by experience. Probably it is a little of each, but it does have the persuasive advantage of just happening to work quite well.

We will outline two methods of charting in this chapter, Bar Charts and Point & Figure Charts. A third technique, the use of moving averages, perhaps more logically belongs in Chapter 11, and hence is covered there.

It should be stressed that this brief chapter can only hope to cover the basic techniques used in technical analysis; many analysts have spent years refining their techniques and learning to interpret charts. Such experience is not acquired by any other means than by actual application to real markets over a period of time. Regrettably, one cannot be taught to play tennis by reading about the game alone; one must also pay tennis!

10.4   Bar Charts

Bar charts are simple to construct. Price is plotted on the vertical scale of a sheet of graph paper and the horizontal scale is time, usually marked off in days. Each day a vertical line is drawn representing the price range experienced during the day, with its top at the day's high and its bottom at the day's low. A horizontal mark, 'the closing tick', is made across the bar at the price at which the market closed for the day. Charts 1–9 shown in this chapter are bar charts. Some of the

CHART 1

BAR

CHART

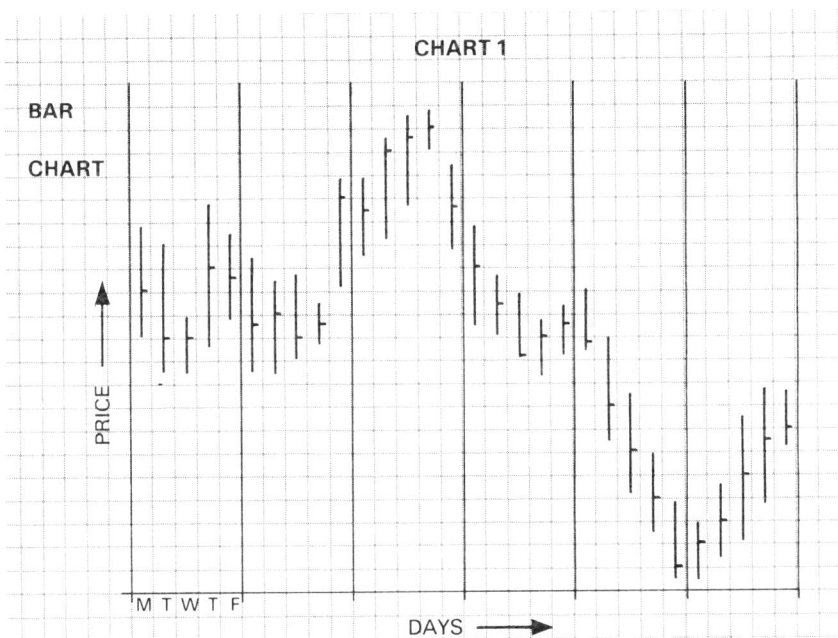

M T W T F

DAYS ⟶

charts shown omit the closing ticks in the interests of clarity.

An important concept in chart interpretation is that of 'support and resistance'. It will often be found that a price rises to a particular level where the market judges it to be high enough, and so profit-taking sets in, causing a fall back. Buyers now come in, feeling the currency to be cheap, but perhaps are reluctant to continue to hold it when the previous high is neared, so that the cycle repeats. A pattern of successive highs at more or less the same level is thus built up. (See Chart 2). This level is termed a 'resistance level'; prices may bounce down from it time and again. There is said to be resistance to prices going higher. Eventually in such a situation prices may break through

CHART 2

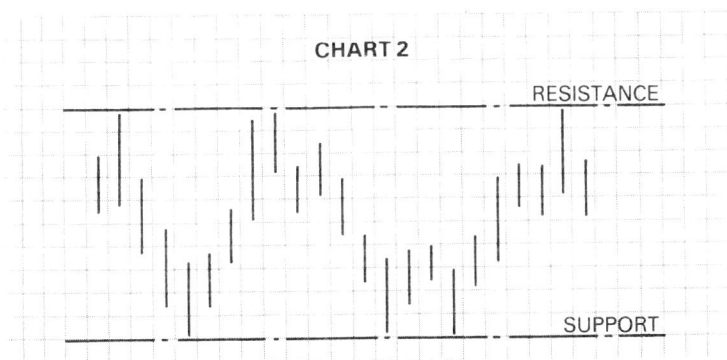

RESISTANCE

SUPPORT

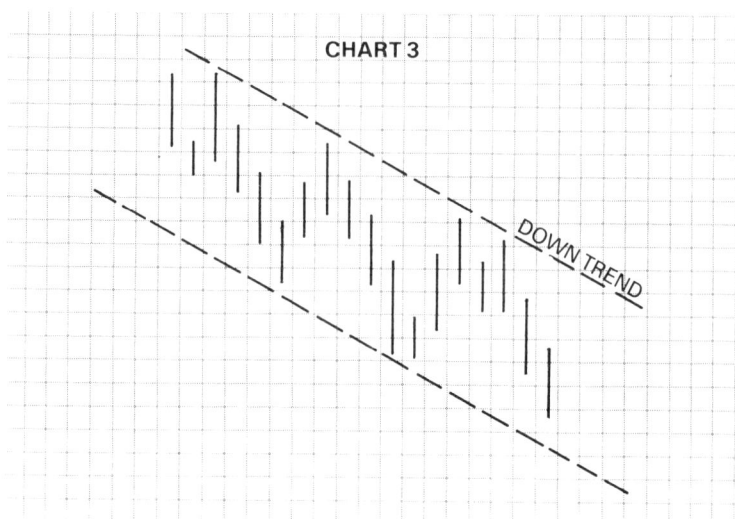

CHART 3

DOWN TREND

the resistance level, and if this occurs it is a very significant move – chartists would expect a substantial further upward move once the resistance level has been penetrated.

Chartists would also expect that, in due course, when prices fall again, the former resistance level may prove 'hard to get through' on the way down – it now becomes a level of 'support', providing an expected temporary floor for the price. Support levels are the exact converse of resistance levels, being levels that prices fail to penetrate on successive occasions when attempting to move downwards. A classic alternate support and resistance pattern is shown in Chart 2.

Support and resistance lines do not have to be horizontal. One of the oldest chart techniques is to draw a straight line connecting the highs on a bar chart, and a second straight line connecting the lows to identify 'trend channels'. (See Chart 3). If the two lines are roughly parallel, then:

a: If they slope down, the top line is considered the significant line and is regarded as a sloping resistance line. Whilst the bars continue below this line then the downtrend is intact, but if the closing price penetrates this line then the downtrend is assumed to be over and a new uptrend is possibly about to start.

CHART 4

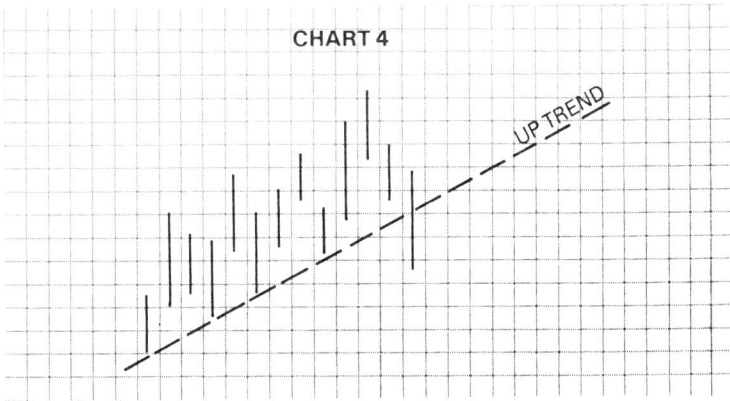

b: If the two lines slope up, then the bottom line is considered the significant line and becomes a sloping support line. The penetration of this line, as shown in Chart 4, signals the end of the uptrend.

Trend line penetration is only one way to identify possible trend reversals. A second is to look for the specific patterns that often seem to be associated with such reversals. There are many of these, but three of them arise particularly frequently and are distinctive in appearance.

a: 'Double Top'
See Chart 5. Self explanatory. A 'Double Bottom' is simply an inverted 'Double Top' and makes a low.

CHART 5

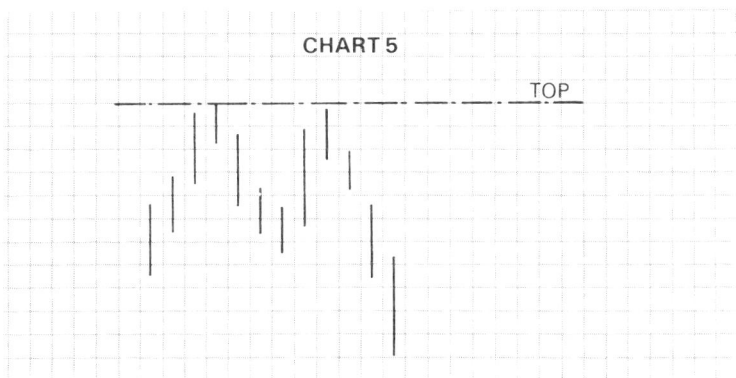

CHART 6

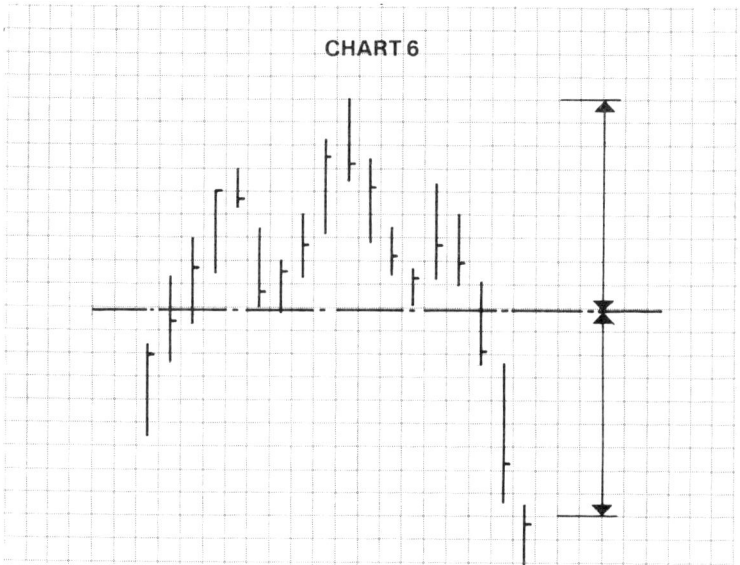

b: 'Head & Shoulders'
See Chart 6. Three peaks with the central one higher than the other two. A classic reversal pattern which often follows a fast moving rise in a market. Once the 'neckline' (shown here chain dotted) is penetrated a fall equal to the head to neckline distance is indicated. Again, the head and shoulders bottom is the same pattern inverted.

c: 'Island Bottom'
See Chart 7. The bottom formation is separated from the preceding and following bars by a clear vertical gap, leaving an 'island' at the bottom. Island tops also occur.

CHART 7

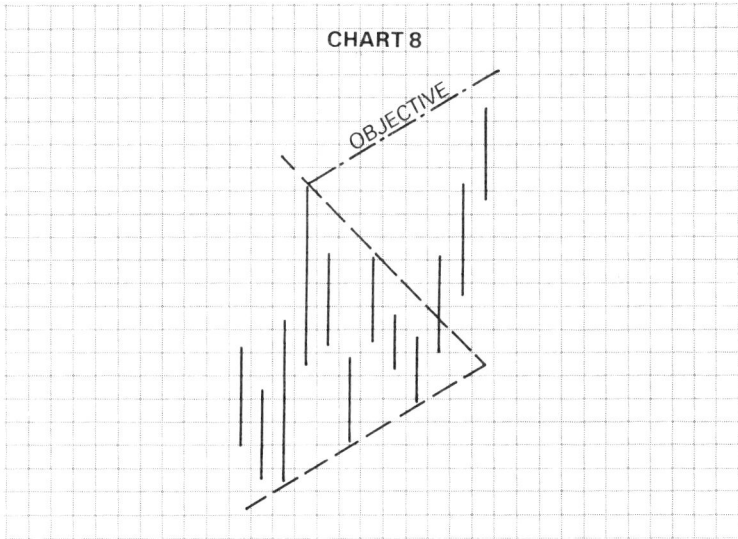

CHART 8

OBJECTIVE

Convergent trendlines create 'triangles'. These may be:

a: roughly symmetrical about the horizontal axis as in Chart 8, or

b: descending triangles with a descending top line and a horizontal base as in Chart 9, or

c: ascending triangles with an ascending bottom line and a horizontal top.

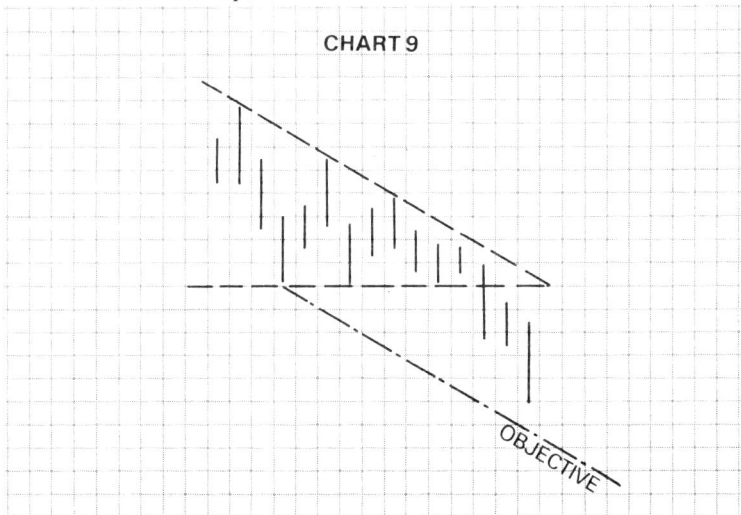

CHART 9

OBJECTIVE

Symmetrical triangles are symptomatic of a nervous market, with traders uncertain which way to jump. Breakout from the triangle may be either way, but when it comes it may signal a major move, the scale of which is indicated by the 'objective' shown on Chart 8. A descending triangle 'expects' an eventual downward break, with an objective as shown in Chart 9. An ascending triangle similarly 'expects' an upward break.

It should be noted that beginner chartists are apt to spot triangles everywhere, some of which are imaginary! Remember that at least three bars touching the presumed triangle are necessary to identify it, but preferably four or five.

Experienced chartists will use many other 'classic patterns' than those introduced here; flags, wedges, keys, gaps, and many more. Those wishing to explore this topic in greater depth are referred to the bibliography.

10.5   Point & Figure Charts

Another form of chart frequently used by market operators, particularly to assess timing decisions within periods as short as an hour or a day, is the oddly named Point & Figure Chart. The unusual features of this type of chart is that there is no horizontal time scale, although price forms the vertical scale as in bar charts. This vertical price scale is divided into equal units (called boxes), whose size is chosen so as to constitute the smallest price movement that the chartist wishes to show. (That is, movements smaller than one box would not be of interest.)

By convention, periods of rising prices are plotted as a vertical column of X's, and periods of falling prices are plotted as a vertical column of O's. (See Chart 10.) So long as prices continue to rise X's will continue to be added to the top of the existing column of X's; when prices turn round, the next column is started, beginning with an O diagonally down from the top X. O's will now be plotted down this column until the price ceases to fall. When this happens and the price turns up again, a new column of X's is started, beginning with an X diagonally up from the lowest O, and so on. So far, so good, but what constitutes a reversal?

The most common Point & Figure reversal convention is the so-called '3 Box Reversal Method'. To illustrate this, suppose we are in an uptrend. We are putting additional X's on top of the existing

CHART 10

POINT &

FIGURE

CHART

PRICE ↑

```
                                          X
                                          X O
                                          X O
                        X   X         X   X O
                        X O X O       X O X O           X   X   X
                        X O   O       X O X O           X O X O X O
                        X     O     X   X O   O       X   X O X O   O
                X   X     O     X O X     O           X O X O
                X O X     O X   X O X     O           X O X
                X O X     O X O X O X     O           X O X
                X O       O X O X     O X       X   X X O
                X         O X O X     O X O X   X O X O X
                          O   O X     O   O X O X O X O
                              O X         O   O X O
                              O                 O
```

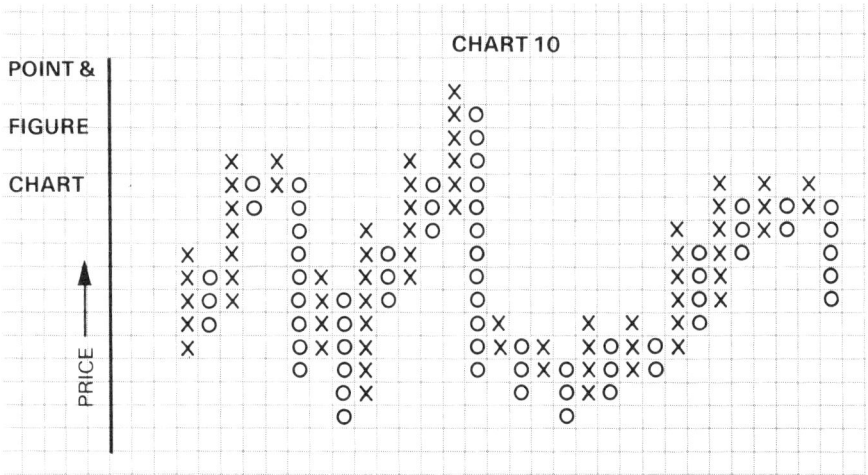

column of X's each time the price rises into a new box. When the uptrend falters and no new high is made, then the analyst will check whether the low since the last X was entered is three boxes below that X. If so, then a 3 Box Reversal has occurred and a new O column is started diagonally down from the top X. But unless the reversal is at least three boxes no new plot is made.

Point & Figure charts exhibit the same support and resistance patterns as Bar charts, which since the vertical price scale is identical for both types of chart is perhaps not too surprising. Chart 11 shows the classic Point & Figure buy and sell signals, based on this principle.

For the 'buy' pattern, when the second column of X's goes higher than the previous one (here assumed to have been a resistance level last time round, since prices fell from there) then prices have broken through the resistance level upwards and this will represent a buy signal. The 'sell' signal is simply the mirror image, with the last O

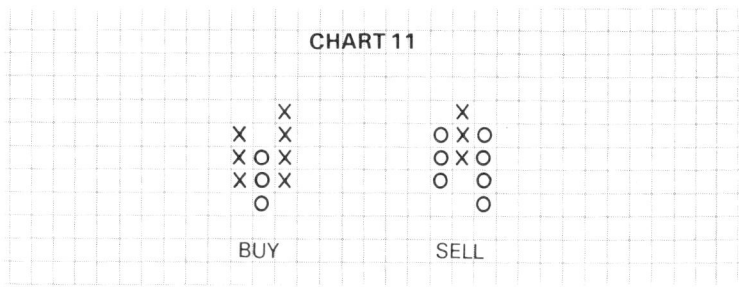

CHART 11

```
          X                 X
      X   X             O X O
      X O X             O X O
      X O X             O   O
        O                   O

      BUY                SELL
```

CHART 12

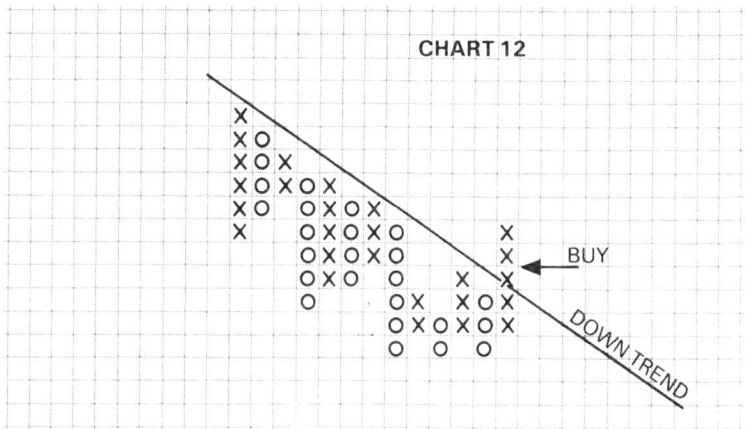

breaking below the support level. Sloping trend lines similarly recur in Point & Figure charts, as for example in the downtrend shown in Chart 12. Penetration of this downtrend provides a buy signal.

Point & Figure chartists can recognise and use many dozens of different classic patterns, which would take us far beyond the scope of this short coverage, but again, those wishing to pursue this somewhat addictive subject are referred to the bibliography.

10.6 Moving Averages

Thus far the chart techniques have been solely concerned with plotting price behaviour as such. Technical analysis begins with the price charts but then goes further, to consider speed of change of price, the strength and direction of underlying trends, and the extent to which the price at any time is out of line with the trend and is thus 'overbought' or 'oversold'.

Derived statistics of various kinds are used to add depth to the basic price data, to highlight unusual situations and to aid the assessment of the market situation. Such statistical devices are known as 'technical indicators'. The most frequently used technical indicators are simple moving averages of the price. For instance, the 6 day moving average is a straight average of the price on each of the last 6 trading days. Moving averages are used to indicate trends as their construction causes short term fluctuations about the trend to cancel out, leaving a 'pure' trend. The period of the average is chosen by the analyst according to the time horizon he is interested in, and averages anywhere between 3 days and 150 days may be used for different purposes. Shorter averages are relevant to short term traders, longer ones when the longer term trend is of more interest. Since moving averages are trend followers they may be used as though they were curved lines of support and resistance, and so treated as a means to provide and sell signals whenever a price line crosses a moving average. This aspect is treated in detail in Chapter 11.

Unlike pattern recognition, methods based on moving averages give no indication of the likely size of movements that might occur, but they do provide confirmation of the turning points in trend lines that must necessarily occur at tops and bottoms.

10.7   Oscillators

Oscillators or momentum indicators measure the rate of change of prices. Various types of formula are used to achieve this:

a: Price today/price X days earlier × 100.

b: Price/Xday moving average × 100.

c: Short moving average/longer moving average × 100.

d: Price – moving average/moving average × 100.

All these oscillators (with the exception of type *d*) average 100 over time, with a band width about that figure which may be established by experience. Bands are not necessarily symmetrical about 100. In general, an oscillator at the top of its typical range indicates an overbought condition and so expects a price fall towards the trend line, and correspondingly, an oscillator at or near the lower end of its typical range indicates an oversold condition.

A price line will cut the moving average line at a turning point in a trend (that is, price will fall from above the moving average to below it at a market top), a phenomenon known as 'crossover'. Similarly, a short moving average will crossover a longer moving average at a turning point. It will be seen that the make up of the oscillators serves to pick up these crossovers in a statistical, numeric, form rather than the visual way in which a pure chartist would arrive at this result. The chartist would actually draw out the two graphs and observe them approaching one another and then crossing over. The calculation arrives at the ratio of the two figures, with crossover occurring when the ratio is at 100%.

Experienced analysts will follow charts, averages and oscillators and use each of the presentations of the data to glean more about the behaviour of the market. It is this process of looking at a number of different aspects in combination that enables some of the more frequent pitfalls to be avoided. Which leads directly to the important matter of confirmation.

10.8   Confirmation

Any single chart or technical method is liable to throw up a number of 'false' results from time to time – a double top is likely to be a price peak, but is not certainly so, merely highly likely. Technical analysts will thus tend to reason as follows. It *looks* like a top formation, but is it confirmed by other data available to me? Has the fall to date taken the price through the support line? Has the price crossed a moving average? Is the moving average falling? Do the oscillators indicate an overbought condition? On fundamental economic criteria would it be expected that the price should in fact be moving downwards?

In summary, in what ways can the analyst confirm his initial tentative opinion that he is seeing the beginnings of a turning point? The important thing here is that the analyst must avoid leaping to instant conclusions based on one technical indication alone; the more ways in which he can obtain confirmation of his initial hunch, the greater is the probability that he will come up with the correct answer.

10.9   Self Delusion

This aspect is merely the corollary of the need for confirmation. It is frighteningly easy to believe a chart indication merely because it happens to fit in with one's current ideas as to what the market 'ought' to be doing, and thus to dispense with the need to wait a while for confirmation to materialise. When confirmation fails to turn up it is a human reaction not to wish to pay much attention to that fact but to persist with the earlier view. When this is the scenario, one is usually wrong!

Equally, when perhaps at risk on a currency position it is tempting to focus upon those indicators favourable to the view taken and to discount those stubbornly pointing the other way. This is an equally hazardous self delusion; if an indicator suggests that the position be cut, even if at a loss, it is usually wisest/cheapest to simply cut. Technical methods are objective, factual and unbiased; if full value is to be extracted from them, then the evidence they submit must be weighed with cold-eyed objectivity too.

11 Technical Trading

11.1 Controlling the Size of the Risk Taken

First we will consider this aspect from the point of view of deciding an appropriate level of foreign exchange exposure. Some companies operate a house rule to the effect that they will cover all exposures forward as soon as known; others never cover forward at all and take the swings of the market as best they can. But most companies try to be selective, covering or not as they think will give the best result on that occasion. Unfortunately many of the methods employed to take these decisions are somewhat *ad hoc*, and can produce highly unsatisfactory results. This chapter suggests some systematic ways of approaching these decisions. There are really two basic decisions involved here, whether to deal and, if 'yes', when to deal.

11.2 Caution and the 20% Rule

Selective cover is about deliberate decisions to leave certain risks uncovered. This necessarily means that the company's information system must be good enough to identify all existing exposures and the control system must be capable of operating the company AT ZERO CURRENCY RISK. Dealing decisions then become concerned with the economics of CONTROLLED DEVIATIONS from this zero position. Accidental or 'uncoverable' exposures are not part of selective cover since they are involuntary.

Decisions to leave certain risks uncovered inevitably means that there is a possibility of a wrong judgment and a resultant loss. It is vital that the company DECIDES IN ADVANCE THE SIZE OF THE MAXIMUM TOLERABLE LOSS that it can contemplate in such an event and that the selective cover policy operates within this restraint.

The size of the tolerable loss will typically be set in relation to the company's capital base, profitability and cash position, and also by reference to the company's style of operating: conservative or aggressive. It was established in Chapter 1 that currencies typically move 20% in a year, not as a worst case, but as an average. One suggestion therefore, is to use a 20% swing as the basis for setting the maximum currency position that can be run without breaching the company's maximum loss limit. That is, suppose the Board sets a maximum allowable loss of $1,000,000 then this implies a maximum uncovered currency position of $5,000,000. Thus, in the event of encountering the 20% loss on the $5,000,000 the maximum will be touched but not exceeded.

It can be argued that 20% is not the correct figure in many situations. Nor is it; the point is that treasurers should calculate a figure that seems logical to them in their situation and be able to defend their choice of figure by reasoned argument. The problems really arise when there is no defined maximum currency position and then rates start to move rapidly in the wrong direction.

In the situation above, it follows that if the company enters into transactions that create an exposure of, say, $15,000,000 then the treasurer should immediately cover the first $10,000,000 NO MATTER WHAT HE THINKS MARKET RATES WILL DO. His only discretion is to decide where the exposure should be within the band +$5m to −$5m. So he has to hedge until the position gets down to his tolerable level, and then manage the net position as best he can. If he gets everything wrong, the firm loses $1m, (and possibly its treasurer too!), but the firm is unlikely to lose more than it originally was prepared to accept as its worst case. So how does the treasurer set about this task of managing the net $5m?

This is a matter that requires much more than a view of whether or not to take out cover, it also concerns the timing aspect of when to take out cover, and equally importantly, when to cease to cover. These timing aspects require quite different techniques, and these we turn to next.

11.3 Moving Averages

There are a number of occasions when it may be felt attractive to continue to run an open position in the expectation of gains. The problem immediately arises as to the level at which the position should be cut out. The problem is particularly difficult since markets tend to move in an untidy zig-zag pattern rather than in continuous smooth curves, and short term fluctuations may be wide enough to obscure the trend. The treasurer's permanent dilemma may be illustrated thus: If the market moves against us, is it just part of the

		MOVING AVERAGES	
Day	Price	4 day ave	8 day ave
1	95		
2	90		
3	87		
4	81	88·25	
5	82	85	
6	76	81·5	
7	79	79·5	
8	73	77·5	82·875
9	68	74	79·5
10	64	71	76·25
11	60	66·25	72·875
12	59	62·75	70·125
13	56	59·75	66·875
14	55	57·5	64·25
15	57	56·75	61·5
16	59	56·75	59·75
17	55	56·5	58·125
18	55	56·5	57
19	58	56·75	56·75
20	60	57	56·875
21	63	59	57.75
22	65	61·5	59
23	66	63·5	60·125
24	64	64·5	60·75
25	70	66·25	62·625
26	80	70	65·75
27	90	76	69·75
28	87	81·75	73·125
29	93	87·5	76·875
30	90	90	80

normal zig-zag path, with the trend still heading our way, or is it a true market turn? And how can we identify which it is?

The normal statistical device used to separate out the trend is a moving average. A straight average is taken of the last x days opening (or closing) prices and this average is used as a trend indication. Use of this type of short term moving average will take out the zig-zag patterns of a typical price chart and produce a substantially smooth 'trend' line. This is, at the very least, helpful in visualising what is happening – it is a means of sorting out the wood from the trees.

The table on p. 134 and the graph below illustrate the idea well. They show a daily price, a 4 day moving average (i.e. the average of today's price and the previous 3 days), and an 8 day moving average. It is apparent that even an average as short as 4 days is able to 'ride'

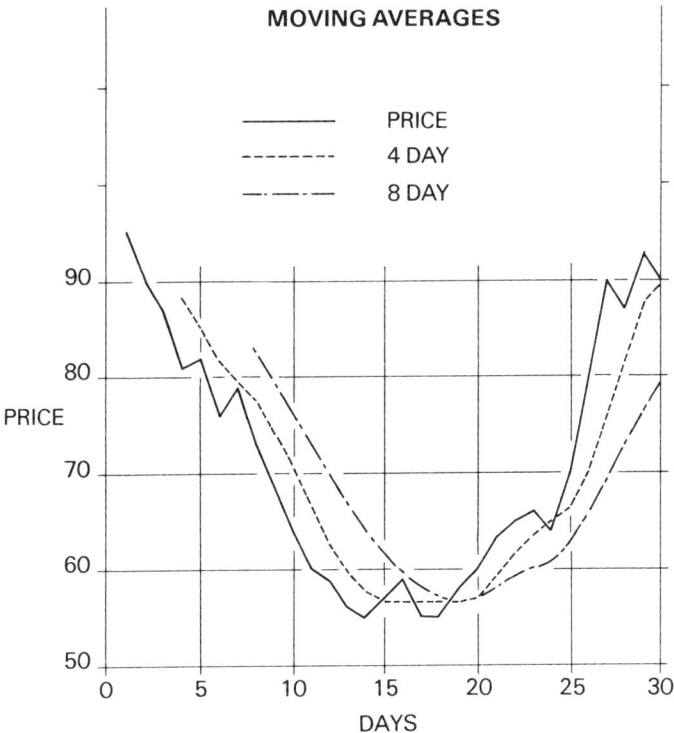

MOVING AVERAGES

——————— PRICE

- - - - - - - 4 DAY

—·—·— 8 DAY

PRICE

DAYS

minor zig-zags in the price pattern to a useful extent. For instance, the zig-zag in days 4 to 8 results in no change in the steady downtrend shown by the 4 day average – when the rate moves up on individual days the average nonetheless moves steadily downwards, suggesting that these day to day fluctuations do not constitute turning points in the underlying trend.

11.4 Trend Reversal Indicators

The example shows a typical trend reversal pattern; a steady downtrend reaches its low and, after forming a bottom pattern, commences to establish an equally clear uptrend. Or at least, now that we can see the entire pattern drawn out and can use perfect hindsight, it is a 'clear uptrend'. It may not be as clear as this at the time. This is where the true usefulness of the moving average technique comes into play: we can use the averages to confirm whether or not we have reached the end of the downtrend. In fact we can identify the 'turn' in a large number of ways. For the moment simply observe that:

> *a*: During the downtrend the price line is always below the 4 day average.
>
> *b*: During the downtrend the 4 day average is always below the 8 day average.
>
> *c*: During the uptrend the price line is always above the 4 day average.
>
> *d*: During the uptrend the 4 day average is always above the 8 day average.

A number of tests suggest themselves that might be expected to signal the end of a downtrend.

> *a*: If the 4 day average turns up (occurs day 19)
>
> *b*: If the price goes above the 4 day average (occurs day 15 & 19)
>
> *c*: If the 8 day average turns up (occurs day 20)
>
> *d*: If the price goes above the 8 day average (occurs day 19)
>
> *e*: If the 4 day average goes above the 8 day average (occurs day 20)

As will be seen by study of the graph, *any* of these tests will work quite well, with different degrees of speed and sensitivity, and they do so at *the time.* The precise length of average that works 'best' and the particular rule adopted from those suggested above will vary from market to market and have to be found by experiment over a period, using historical price data. The above example merely illustrates the principles involved.

11.5 Stop Loss Orders

The basic idea behind the 'Stop Loss Order' is very simple. A trader having a position, say long of a particular currency, will protect himself against any sudden fall by placing a sell order at a level somewhat below the current market level. If that level is reached the sell order is triggered. The existence of the order limits his loss to this 'acceptable' amount and 'stops loss' beyond that. If the stop loss level is not reached the position remains in place.

Some professional traders routinely set a stop loss level every time they enter into an open position, placing a stop loss sell order simultaneously with their purchase order. If their position improves they move the stop loss level up from time to time in order to lock in successive slices of their unrealised gain. This provides a semi-automatic way of adhering to the old trader's adage: 'run a profit, but cut a loss.'

11.6 Moving Stop Loss Orders

The interesting idea now arises of using the moving averages as an automatic means of setting stop loss levels, moving the stop loss level every day in line with some selected average. As we have seen, at the end of a trend the price line will cut the moving average line; if the moving average were actually related to the stop loss, then the position should cut out close to, but not at, the end of the trend, that is near the 'turn' of the market. Which is exactly what we are trying to achieve.

Before launching into this kind of system there are a few safeguards which have to be observed:

  a: We do not want normal daily price volatility to cut out the position unnecessarily.

  b: It is usually considered to be especially necessary to limit loss tightly in the early days of a new exposure.

MOVING STOP LOSS LEVELS

Day	Price	4 day ave	Stop
1	95		98
2	90	96	98
3	87	92	95
4	81	88·25	91
5	82	85	88
6	76	81·5	84
7	79	79·5	82
8	73	77·5	80
9	68	74	77
10	64	71	74
11	60	66·25	69
12	59	62·75	65
13	56	59·75	62
14	55	57·5	60
15	57	56·75	59
16	59	56·75	59 cut?
17	55	56·5	59
18	55	56·5	59
19	58	56·75	59
20	60	57	59 cut
21	63	59	
22	65	61·5	
23	66	63·5	
24	64	64·5	
25	70	66·25	
26	80	70	
27	90	76	
28	87	81·75	
29	93	87·5	
30	90	90	

We can handle these considerations as follows. Assuming we have been following a particular market for some while, we will have established the typical size of a daily movement. For the market used in our moving averages example let us say this typical variation is 3 points. We now set out parameters for running a simple moving stop loss system below. (We assume we believe we are in a falling market and wish to go short.)

MOVING 'STOP LOSS'

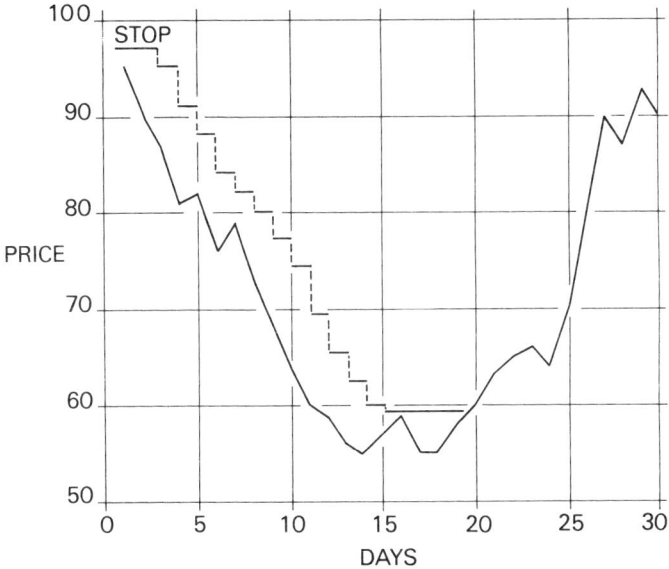

a: We will set the stop loss level at:
  (i) 3 points above the price we sold at, or
  (ii) 3 points over a chosen moving average (for the sake of the example we will use the four day average) Whichever is the lower.

b: Whilst we have a short position we will only move the stop down in accordance with (ii) above, but NEVER UP.

c: We will only cut the position if/when the stop is triggered, otherwise we will continue to run it.

Let us try out this fairly primitive system on the data in our example, assuming that we sell on the first day at a price of 95, and thereafter simply follow the system. The initial stop loss level will be 98 (from rule *a* (i)). The stop level for the subsequent days until the position is cut is shown in the table, and graphically in the diagram entitled 'Moving Stop Loss'.

The power of this technique is quite apparent, and would result in a gain of some 35 points assuming a cut out at around the level of 60, against a best possible cut out level of 55. Although the method will never cut out at the bottom, it will always do so close to the bottom. Note that although the 4 day average rises on days 19 and 20 the stop is held down, following rule (b), and so causes the cut out.

The limitations of the technique should also be pointed out, lest it be thought that we have hit upon some wonderful panacea, which sadly of course we have not!

a: Little guidance is provided as to when to take up a position, as opposed to when to close an existing position. Of course, if the averages are above the price line it is an indication that prices have been falling; but it does not necessarily mean they will continue to do so. The decision to enter into a position would normally rest on some separately derived forecasts concerning the currency.

b: Stop loss orders limit loss, they do not eliminate it. If the position is the wrong way round in the first place the method may limit the extent of the resultant loss (and tend to lead to speedier cut out of bad positions that might otherwise be held in the hope of improvement), but there will still be a loss.

c: The method is ideal where markets are making substantial moves. Where markets are 'stalled' and are moving broadly sideways the method can lead to a string of small losses. In this situation one can only stay out of the market or use some other method to decide when to hop in and out.

General Bibliography

Foreign Exchange

Brown, B. 'Money Hard and Soft', Macmillan, 1978

Coninx, R. 'Foreign Exchange Today', Woodhead-Faulkner, 1978

Donaldson, A. 'Corporate Currency Risk', *Financial Times*, 1980

Federal Accounting Standards Board, 'Statement of Financial Accounting Standards No. 52', 1981

The Forex Association, 'The London Foreign Exchange Market', 1981

Heywood, J. 'Foreign Exchange and the Corporate Treasurer', A. & C. Black, 1981

Institute of Chartered Accountants, Accounting Standards Committee Exposure Drafts 21, 1977, and 27, 1980.

Kenyon, A. 'Currency Risk Management', Wiley, 1981

Kubarych, R. 'Foreign Exchange Markets in the United States', Federal Reserve Bank of New York, 1978

Mandich, D. 'Foreign Exchange Trading Techniques', American Bankers Association, 1976

Riehl and Rodrigues, 'Foreign Exchange Markets', McGraw Hill, 1977

Swiss Bank Corporation, 'Foreign Exchange and Money Market Operations', 1978

Wainman, D. 'Currency Fluctuation', Woodhead-Faulkner, 1976

Currency Options

Philadelphia Stock Exchange Publications
'Listed Options in Foreign Currencies'
'The Third Dimension in Foreign Exchange'
'Understanding Foreign Currency Options'

The Exchange also publishes a weekly newsletter entitled 'Foreign Currency Options'.

Financial Futures

Chicago Board of Trade Publications
'An Introduction to Financial Futures'
'US Treasury Bond Futures'
'Domestic CD Futures'
Continental Illinois Bank and Trust Co, 'Financial Instruments Futures', 1978
First Chicago, 'A Way to Manage Interest Rate Risks', 1981
IMM Publications
'The International Money Market'
'Inside Eurodollar Futures'
'Trading in Tomorrows'
'Understanding Futures in Foreign Exchange'
'Opportunities in CD Futures'
LIFFE Publications
'LIFFE – An Introduction'
'LIFFE – Hedging Techniques'
LIFFE/Price Waterhouse Joint Publications
'Financial Futures – Accounting Principles'
'Internal Controls for Financial Futures'
Little, J. 'Financial Futures Hedging Guide', Clayton Brown, 1979
Loosigian, A. 'Interest Rate Futures', Dow Jones, 1980.

Technical Forecasting

Edwards, R. D. and Magee, 'Technical Analysis of Stock Trends', John Magee Inc., Boston, Mass
Gann, W. D. 'How to Make Profits in Commodities', Lambert-Gann Publishing Inc
Gifford, E. 'Money Making Matters', Exchange Buildings Commodity Syndicate, Warwick
Sklarew, A. 'Techniques of a Professional Commodity Chart Analyst', Commodity Research Bureau, Liberty Plaza, NY

Glossary

The appended glossary is intended partly to define the many specialist words used in this book, but it also includes a great number of terms used by market dealers in their daily work. The words selected range from precise technical terms, through useful shorthands, down to plain market slang. It is not really necessary to know many of these but they are included because the reader may come across them when talking to dealers.

Foreign Exchange Markets

Answerback: Code name of a telex subscriber, printed automatically by the telex machine at the start and finish of every message. Answerbacks are unique to the individual user and are used to identify the caller.

Arbitrage: 1. Dealing between two centres to make a turn in the rate due to a temporary difference in rates between the two places.

2. Creating funds in one currency by borrowing another and converting to that required by means of a swap deal.

Band: Maximum permitted range of fluctuation of a given currency against a reference currency according to an existing international agreement.

Bankers Payment: Payment order issued by a bank on behalf of its customer. A recipient of a bankers payment looks to the issuing bank for funds, not its customer, so the issuing bank will check that its customer has adequate funds or credit first. Bankers payments may be sent by mail or by telex transfer.

Base Currency: Every exchange rate consists of a quoted currency quoted against a base currency. The base currency is usually the dollar or sterling, e.g. in a French franc quote of 4·93 60/70 French francs per dollar the franc is the quoted currency, the base currency is the dollar.

Bid: Quote at which dealer buys or borrows currency.

Bid Market: Temporary situation where bids exceed offers at the present market rate.

Big Figure: The second figure after the decimal point in a price quotation. If the French franc rate against the dollar is 4·91 60/70 the big figure is one.

Bretton Woods: Agreement made at Bretton Woods, New Hampshire, USA, in July 1944. The agreement, signed by 44 nations, was designed to provide a stable monetary environment to facilitate the economic reconstruction of the world after World War 2. The agreement established the International Monetary Fund, and set up a fixed rate system of foreign exchange rates for nearly all the principal currencies of the world.

Broken Date, Odd Date: Interbank dealing is usually for fixed periods of 1, 2, 3 or 6 months with 12 months a standard period in some currencies. Any other value date (such as 4 months 6 days) is a 'broken date'.

Broker: Brokers match buyers and sellers, or borrowers and lenders, in the interbank market and receive a commission 'brokerage', for so doing.

Brokerage, 'Bro': Commission charge to a bank by a broker.

Broker's Line: Direct telephone line between a broker's office and a bank's dealing room.

Broker's slip: Form sent from a broker to a bank, noting details of a deal transacted by the bank via the broker, and claiming brokerage.

Business Day: Day other than a weekend or public holiday in the city concerned. In most western countries Saturday is not a business day in foreign exchange markets. However, in Arabia Saturdays and Sundays are both business days but Friday is not.

Buying Rate: The rate at which the bank buys the quoted currency.

Cable: The spot exchange rate between US dollar and sterling, e.g. 'cable is now 1·74 20/22'. This term arises from the early days of the market when a cable was sent from New York to London each day to advise the level at which the dollar was trading against sterling in New York.

Cash: Banknotes, coin, and traveller's cheques.

Certificate of Deposit (CD): A certificate issued by a bank against currency deposited. The certificate entitles the bearer to the principal plus interest at the maturity date.

Changes: Used by dealers on telex, when a rate previously quoted changes, to indicate they are no longer prepared to deal at the old rate, e.g.

Bank A 'spot and fwds marks pls'

Bank B '2·32 70/75

  53–47

  99–93

 152–146

 320–310

changes spot now 72–77'

Concertation: Daily liaison between the central banks of the EEC countries and the non-EEC participants in the snake, to consult as to intervention policies.

Confirmation: Written advice from one counterparty in a deal to the other in which the main facts of the deal are confirmed. These would include: date on which deal done, amount plus currency dealt, whether purchase or sale, value date, agreed rate, etc. It may or may not include payment instructions.

Convertible Currency: A currency having a reasonably adequate international market through which it may be readily converted into any other currency.

Copey: Market slang for Danish krone.

Counterparty: A principal in a foreign exchange deal.

Countervalue: Where, in a foreign exchange deal, a principal buys DM500,000 against dollars at a rate of 2·40 the countervalue is $208,333·33.

Country Cheque: Any sterling cheque drawn on UK bank other than a Town cheque, which see.

Cover: 1. To take out forward contracts to protect against exchange fluctuation between today's date and the due payment date.
2. To lay off.

Currency Clause: A price clause in an export contract which, for instance, specifies that the sterling sum payable for the goods shall vary in line with the market exchange rate for Swedish kronor against sterling, so as to maintain a constant value in Swedish kronor.

Deal: A single transaction in foreign exchange. A customer calling his bank and effecting forward cover for a series of four payments due under a commercial contract, will do four 'deals', one for each date.

Dealing Board: The panel of communications equipment forming part of a dealer's desk.

Dealing Slip: Slip written out by dealer to record the deal he has done. It will show the name of the counter-party, the amount, currency, and value date, whether purchase or sale, agreed rate, and the dealer's name. It may or may not also include instructions depending on the system used by the particular bank.

Deposit Book: The net position arising from all deposit and loan transactions in a given currency.

Depot: Deposit, e.g. Depot Market = Deposit Market.

Depth of Market: Extent to which transactions may easily be placed in the market without causing disturbance to the rate. See 'Thin market', 'Stable market'.

Details: See Instructions.

Discount: A negative premium. See Premium.

DM DMark: Deutsche Mark.

Domestic Credit Expansion (D.C.E.): A measure of money supply designed to indicate the change in the money supply available for use within the domestic economy. In the UK, approximately equal to change in M3 minus balance of payments surplus (or plus deficit) in period.

Drawdown: Of loans. The drawdown is the actual payment of the loan to the borrower. This may be at a much later date than when the loan was arranged.

Either Way Price: A quote with a spread of zero. Buying rate the same as selling price.

EMS: European Monetary System – see Snake.

Escalator Clause: Clause on a medium term capital project (such as construction of a power station) to increase the money sum payable to the contractor in line with inflation.

Eurocurrency: A deposit account in any major market currency where the owner of the funds is a non-resident of the country of the currency.

Eurodollar: A dollar deposit owned by someone other than a resident of the USA.

Exchange Control: Regulations restricting or forbidding certain types of foreign currency transactions by nationals.

Exotic Currencies, Exotics: Currencies not having a developed international market, and which are infrequently dealt.

Exposure, Accounting: The effect on a company resulting from a movement in a particular currency as it would show up in financial accounts.

Exposure, Economic: The economic effect on a company resulting from a movement in a particular currency.

Exposure, Transaction: Exposure arising from the currency cash flow of the company in the short term, say the next year.

Exposure, Translation: Exposure arising from the translation of the currency balance sheets upon consolidation of foreign subsidiaries.

Federal Reserve System: The system of twelve regional Federal Reserve Banks in the USA which carry out the role of a Central Bank. The twelve Federal Reserve Banks are: Boston, New York, Philadelphia, Cleveland, Richmond, Atlanta, Chicago, St Louis, Minneapolis, Kansas City, Dallas and San Francisco.

Fed. Target Range: The range of growth in monetary aggregates that is aimed at by Federal Reserve policy, e.g. 'Fed. Target Range for growth of M1' is currently 7–10% per annum. The means to this end may be another target range – e.g. 'the Fed. target rate for the interest rate on Fed. Funds is $5\frac{3}{4}$% to 6%'.

Firm Quote: Rate given at which the dealer is committed to deal, at least for a normal marketable amount. Often qualified, such as 'Firm for one million'.

Fixed Rate Currency: Currency having a fixed rate of exchange within narrow limits versus another reference currency, usually the dollar, sterling or the French franc.

Floating Rate Currency: Currency having its exchange rate determined by market forces including Central Bank intervention, but having no limits to its fluctuation relative to any reference currency. See Fixed Rate Currency.

FOMC: Federal Open-Market Committee. Committee that co-ordinates policy on sales of US government debt and monetary policy generally on behalf of the Federal Reserve System.

FOMC meetings usually take place on the first Tuesday after the 15th of each month. The directives of the FOMC are made public one month after issue, e.g. the mid-January directive to the 'Manager of the System Open-Market Account' is released to the press in mid-February. Because of this, US monetary policy is open and widely debated by economists.

Foreign Exchange Deal: A contract to exchange one currency for another at an agreed price for settlement on an agreed date.

Forex: Foreign Exchange.

Forward Book: The net position arising from all forward transactions in a given currency.

Forward Contract: Any contract for settlement later than spot date.

Forward–Forward Deal: 1. Simultaneous purchase and sale of one currency for different forward value dates.

2. Simultaneous deposit and loan of one currency for different maturity dates. This effectively provides a deposit to commence on a future date.

Funding Swap: See Arbitrage, 2.

FX: Foreign Exchange.

Group of Ten: A group within the IMF consisting of:

USA	Gt Britain
Germany	France
Italy	Japan
Canada	Netherlands
Belgium	Sweden

Switzerland, not an IMF member, was also assocated with certain key Group of Ten meetings.

Hedge: Action taken by a company to reduce or eliminate a currency exposure. This includes restructuring the balance sheet, taking forward cover to match the exposure on foreign currency assets, and many other techniques.

Hold Account: Current account in a currency other than sterling.

Info Quote: Rate given for information only, without commitment by the dealer to deal at that rate.

Instructions: The specification of the banks at which funds shall be paid and received in settlement of a foreign exchange deal.

Interbank Deal, Market Deal: Deal where both counterparties are banks.

Intervention: Action taken by a Central Bank to influence the rate of exchange of its currency in the market.

Intra Day Limit: Limit set by bank management on the size of each dealer's Intra Day Position.

Intra Day Position: Open position run by a dealer within the day. Usually reduced to square or nearly so before close of business.

Ladder: Dealer's analysis of his forward book or deposit book showing every existing deal by maturity date, and the net position at each future date arising.

Lay Off: To carry out a transaction in the market to offset a previous transaction and return to a square position.

LIBOR: London Interbank Offered Rate. The rate at which principal London banks offer to lend currency (especially dollars) to one another at a given instant. Often used as a base rate for fixing interest rate on bank loans e.g. 'Interest to be fixed at $1\frac{1}{4}\%$ per annum over LIBOR'.

Long: Overbought position. Assets in the currency exceed liabilities.

M1: Narrow definition of money supply. In the UK consists of notes and coin in circulation plus the sterling notice deposits of the private sector.

M2: Measure of money supply used in the USA, defined as M1 + time deposits excluding large CDs.

M3: Broad definition of money supply. In the UK consists of 'Sterling M3', which see, plus the currency deposits of UK residents.

Mandate: Formal authority from a customer to its banker specifying what shall constitute proper instruction for the bank to act on the customer's behalf.

Market Amount: The minimum amount conventionally dealt for between dealing banks either direct or via brokers. Typically a multiple of $1m depending on the currency.

Risk Aversion: Measure of the extent to which a particular enterprise is prepared to tolerate uncovered exchange risk.

Rollover: 1. Extension of a maturing forward contract.
2. Extension of a maturing loan, particularly in medium term Eurocurrency loans. These are often arranged 'for a period of five years with a rollover every 6 months'.

Running a Position: Keeping a long or short open position as a matter of deliberate policy in the hope of a speculative gain.

SDR: Special Drawing Right. A standard basket of five currencies in fixed amounts as defined by the International Monetary Fund.

Selling Rate: The rate at which the bank sells the quoted currency.

Settlement: Payment of funds on the maturity of a foreign exchange contract.

Settlement Limit: Limit on settlement risk for each counterparty.

Settlement Risk: Risk arising on a foreign exchange deal in the event of non-settlement by the counterparty.

Short: Oversold position. Liabilities in the currency exceeds assets.

Short Date: A deal for a broken date within one month after spot date.

Snake: An agreement whereby certain European states have agreed to keep their exchange rates in line with one another within close limits.

Spot: See Value Spot.

Spot Deal: A deal for currency for delivery two business days from today, that is 'value spot'.

Spot Next: A deal from the spot date until the next day, either as a deposit or a swap.

Spread: The difference between the selling price and the buying price. On a quote of 2·41 30/40 the spread is ten points.

Square Position: Purchases and sales in the currency are equal. Also called 'matched book', 'square book', and 'flat book'.

Stable Market: An active, high turnover market, which can absorb substantial transactions without appreciable movement in the price for the currency concerned.

Sterling M3: Broad definition of money supply. In the UK, consists of M1
  + private sector £ time deposits
  + public sector £ notice deposits
  + public sector £ time deposits
  + certificates of deposit issued
See M1, M3.

Stocky: Market slang for Swedish krona.

Swap Deal: A simultaneous spot sale and forward purchase, or a simultaneous spot purchase and forward sale. In discussing swaps a dealer doing a simultaneous spot sale and forward purchase may say, 'I sell and buy the currency' or may refer solely to the forward end of the deal: 'I buy in the three months', or 'I bid the threes'.

Swissy: Market slang for Swiss franc.

Temporal Accounting: Method of calculating Accounting Exposure which translates all balance sheet items which are usually valued at cost at the exchange rate ruling at the time the cost was established, and all other items at current market rate.

Thin Market: A low turnover or nervous market, where an attempt to do a substantial transaction will result in a definite movement in the market rate. Spreads are wide in a thin market as dealers are apprehensive as to the rate at which they will be able to lay off any deal done.

Tom Next: Short for 'from tomorrow to the next day'. A deal from the next business day until the one after, either as a deposit or a swap. Note that on Friday 'tom next' is from Monday to Tuesday.

Town Cheque: A sterling cheque drawn on the City branch of a London clearing bank.

Trade Ticket: See Dealing Slip.

Trader, Dealer: See Deal.

Value Date, Value: The date agreed for settlement of an exchange transaction, e.g. 'OK, that's agreed, we buy the Guilders at 2·41 60 for value October 28', or 'The 18th is a holiday, so we are dealing for value the 19th'.

Value Spot: An exchange deal for settlement two working days from today.

VDU: Visual Display Unit, computer terminal.

Vostro Account: A foreign bank's account with a local bank, e.g. a French bank's £ account with a London bank will be a Vostro account as far as the London bank is concerned. It will also be a Nostro account as far as the French bank is concerned.

Currency Option Markets

Much of the jargon used in this market is 'borrowed' from the foreign exchange or futures markets, and is listed in the glossary sections for those markets. However, some of the terminology is unique to the currency options market and is thus listed in this section.

At the Money: Option whose exercise price is at the current market price of the currency, i.e. stands at breakeven.

Call Option: Option to buy the contract amount of currency at a specified price (the exercise price) in dollars during a specified period of time (until the expiration date).

Closing Trade: A deal matching or closing an existing open position.

Conversion: Combination deal; buying a put, selling a call, and buying the currency outright in the FX market, thus arbitraging between the option and FX markets.

Exercise Price: The price at which the option holder has the right to buy or sell.

Expiration Month: The dates on which options held expire. The Philadelphia Exchange trades for expiration months of March, June, September, and December.

In the Money: Option which, at present prices, has a positive intrinsic value, so that, if exercised, a profit would be realised.

Intrinsic Value: The extent to which, on current market rates, an option would realise a gross profit if exercised. Thus, if the current cash market price for Deutschemark is $0·40, a DM 38 call has an intrinsic value of $·02. Gross profit for reckoning intrinsic value conventionally ignores premium, commission, and other transaction costs.

Notice (of Exercise): Notice from an option holder of his intention to exercise the option held.

Option Buyer/Option Holder: The party who has acquired the rights contained in an option by the payment of a premium to an option seller. The holder has the right, but no obligation, to exercise the option at any time up to the expiry date. The holder of a call option has the right to buy the currency concerned against sale of US dollars; the holder of a put option has the right to sell the currency concerned against purchase of US dollars.

Option Premium: The price paid by an option buyer to an option writer as the consideration for creating the option.

Option Seller/Option Writer: The party who has undertaken against receipt of a premium, to meet the exercise of an option by an option holder under the terms of that option. The writer is required to satisfy the option if and when it is exercised.

Out of the Money: Option which, at present prices, if exercised, a loss would be realised.

Put Option: Option to sell the contract amount of currency at a specified price (the exercise price) in dollars during a specified period of time (until the expiry date).

Reversal: Opposite of a conversion, which see.

Spread: Combination deal; purchase and sale of a call, or purchase and sale of a put. Time spreads have the purchase and sale on different dates, vertical spreads differ in strike price.

Straddle: Combination deal: put and call for the same date and strike price.

Strangle: Same as straddle but with different strike prices on the two halves of the transaction.

Strike Price: Exercise price.

Time Value: Value attributed to an option over and above the intrinsic value, owing to the possibility of the market moving in the buyer's favour at some point during the balance of the time to run until the expiration date. Option price = Intrinsic value + Time value.

Futures Markets

Arbitrage: Simultaneous purchase and sale in two related markets to take advantage of a price differential.

Basis: Price difference between a futures contract and the related instrument in the cash market. More generally, any price difference from a given futures contract.

Break: Sudden fall in price.

Buy on Close: Order to buy at the end of the day's trading at a price within the closing range.

Buy on Opening: Order to buy at the start of the day's trading at a price within the opening range.

Cash Market: Conventional market for securities, deposits or foreign exchange, trading for immediate rather than future settlement.

CFTC: Commodity Futures Trading Commission; US government agency responsible for regulation and supervision of futures markets in the USA.

Chicago Board of Trade: One of the two major futures markets based in Chicago. Also known as CBOT.

Clearing House: Organisation associated with the Exchange which matches purchases and sales, regulates margin payments and arranges settlement procedures. In the case of the LIFFE market these functions are carried out by ICCH.

Clearing Member: Member of the Exchange who is also a member of the Clearing House. It is possible to trade on the Exchange without membership of the Clearing House, but in such a case all the Non-Clearing Member's trades have to be cleared through a Clearing Member.

Closing Range: Price during the period designated as the official close.

Closing Out: Reducing open position to zero by taking out a new trade equal and opposite in all respects to that previously existing.

Contract: Defined unit of trading, e.g. Eurodollar Contracts on LIFFE are $1m per contract.

Contract Month: One of the months available for delivery and for which prices are quoted on the exchange.

Day Order: Order placed for execution on that day. If the order cannot be fulfilled on that day, it lapses.

Day Trading: Trading by jobbing in and out of the market during the day, closing out at the end of each day.

Delivery: Settlement of a futures contract on maturity by actual delivery of the financial instrument or security, or by settlement in cash.

Delivery Price: Price fixed by the Clearing House at which deliveries are to be made.

Equity: Net position of a customer on his Futures Margin Account, i.e. net funds due to the customer if all trades were liquidated at current market prices.

Factor: Conversion factor to convert the price of any particular bond into the standard deliverable bond.

Financial Future: A standard contract between buyer and seller in which the buyer has a binding obligation to buy a fixed amount (the contract size) at a fixed price (the futures price) on a fixed date (the delivery date) of some underlying security.

Floor Broker: Member who acts on a commission basis, trading on behalf of other members.

Hedge: Position taken in the futures market with the intention of obtaining protection from the effects of price changes in the cash market.

ICCH: The International Commodities Clearing House Limited, the Clearing House for LIFFE. It is owned by the London Clearing Banks.

IMM: International Monetary Market. One of the two major futures exchanges in Chicago.

Intercontract Spread: Simultaneous purchase and sale of two different delivery months of the same contract.

Intermarket Spread: Simultaneous purchase and sale of two different futures contracts with the same delivery month.

Inverted Market: A futures market in which the nearer months are selling at premiums to the more distant months.

Leg: One of the two trades forming a spread.

LIFFE: London International Financial Futures Exchange. Pronounced 'life'.

Limit Move: Maximum price movement in one trading session that is permitted. Movement beyond this will result in a suspension of trading while margin calls are made.

Limit Order: Order with restrictions as to execution, usually specifying price or time limits.

Margin: Money paid to the Clearing House as a guarantee of fulfilment of the contract.

Initial Margin is a fixed amount per contract when a new trade is entered into.

Variation Margin is the amount paid or received daily in respect of unrealised gains or losses on existing trades.

Margin Call: A demand for additional money to be paid in owing to an adverse price movement, or because of trades newly entered into.

Mark to Market: The process of revaluing all contracts on daily closing prices and paying or receiving Variation Margin payments.

Market Order: Order for immediate execution at the prevailing market price.

Minimum Price Fluctuation: Smallest possible price change. More usually called a 'tick' or a 'point'.

MIT: Market if Touched. Order that becomes a Market Order if a specified price is touched.

Open Interest: The number of contracts not yet closed out or delivered.

Open Outcry: Dealing by direct verbal bid and offer between traders in a trading pit.

Pit: Physical area where the trader must stand when intending to place futures trades. Trades are not valid unless both parties to the trade are physically within the pit at the time.

Position Trader: Trader who holds positions for periods longer than a day.

Rally: Upward price movement following a decline.

Range: Difference between highest and lowest price in a given time period.

Reaction: Downward price movement following a rise.

Scalper: Trader who jobs in and out of the market very frequently for small turns. Scalpers may have a large daily turnover, and hold positions for periods of time measured in minutes.

Settlement Price: Price based upon the closing range at which the Clearing House will clear trades, base margin calculations and fix delivery prices.

Spread: Simultaneous purchase of one contract and sale of another.

Stop Loss Order: Order to close out an existing trade at a specified price level with the aim of limiting losses.

Straddle: Spread between two dates of the same contract.

Tick: Change in price.

Volume: Number of transactions in a given contract over a specified period of time.